Praise for

COUNTERINTUITIVE

"Naveen Jain demonstrates that extraordinary results require extraordinary thinking. In *Counterintuitive*, he delivers a masterclass in challenging assumptions and building ideas that create meaningful impact."

—Jay Shetty, *New York Times* bestselling author
and host of the *On Purpose* podcast

"Guided by his belief that our only limit is our imagination, Naveen teaches us how to ask questions that other people don't, challenge the foundations of our thinking, and achieve great things that few would dare to attempt. *Counterintuitive* is an essential read for anyone willing to go against the grain and challenge convention in the pursuit of their dreams."

—Jim Kwik, the Brain Coach, founder of Kwik Learning
and *New York Times* bestselling author of *Limitless*

"Naveen has already improved millions of lives, including my own. His new book, *Counterintuitive*, will help you to improve your life too."

—Paris Hilton, CEO of 11:11 Media, icon, entrepreneur, musician,
producer, creative visionary, innovator, investor, and advocate

"An essential read for anyone looking to break free from conventional thinking and shoot for the moon. Naveen lays out the blueprint for a life less ordinary."

—Peter H. Diamandis, MD, founder and executive
chair of XPRIZE and Fountain Life

COUNTERINTUITIVE

COUNTERINTUITIVE

Unconventional Principles for Success in Life and Business

NAVEEN JAIN

HARRIMAN HOUSE
www.harriman-house.com

First published in 2026 by Harriman House, an imprint of Pan Macmillan
EU Representative: Macmillan Publishers Ireland Ltd, 1st Floor, The Liffey Trust Centre, 117-126 Sheriff Street Upper, Dublin 1, D01 YC43
Associated companies throughout the world
www.panmacmillan.com

British Library Cataloguing in Publication Data
A CIP catalogue record for this book can be obtained from the British Library.

03

Printed and bound by CPI Group (UK) Ltd.
Cover design by Charlotte Smith. Adobe Stock images used.

CONTENTS

INTRODUCTION

MOST PEOPLE ASPIRE to live an extraordinary life, achieving great success in business, relationships, and more. But most of us also recognize that extraordinary results don't come from ordinary, conventional thinking—they come from thinking *counterintuitively*, and then applying that thinking to the real world in new and creative ways.

You might think that this way of thinking, and the ability to apply it, is a gift reserved only for a few exceptional individuals, but the good news is that anyone, no matter how ordinary, can become extraordinary by learning to think differently.

Every day, the average person has 60,000 to 70,000 thoughts. *I want a cup of tea. I wonder if it will rain. Has anyone thought of mining the Moon?* Our thoughts are a cascading deluge of mixed-up notions that, for the most part, are at worst harmful, are often useless, and are at best functional and unremarkable.

Yet, somewhere in all those firing synapses, the brain might generate a fleetingly good idea. *Mining the Moon? Huh. Mining the Moon!* Some of these thoughts might even qualify as *great* ideas, and these are the seeds of innovation and the origin of products, services, and movements that can reshape humanity for the better.

The problem is, very few of these rare, *truly* exceptional sparks result in the thinker *acting* on them.

But when a person dares to question—to be counterintuitive

about—what everyone else takes for granted, the extraordinary becomes possible.

Why should you become counterintuitive?

Imagine if more great ideas had a chance to survive. What if more people took action on their novel ideas because they had a clear process to validate them and bring them to life? What if *your* idea—the one you think is too crazy—survived and became something humanity truly needs? It could be the next big idea that revolutionizes an area you care deeply about, whether it's education, healthcare, the environment, or some other vital aspect of our world.

If you're thinking, *Wait, I thought this book was about counterintuitive thinking, I'm not looking to revolutionize an industry, just to live a better life*, stay with me. Whatever brought you to this book—whether you're striving for personal growth, professional achievement, or global impact—counterintuitive thinking is the key to making it happen.

To achieve extraordinary success, you can't simply follow the well-trodden paths of the majority. Doing what everyone else does only ever leads to ordinary results. But you're reading this book, I assume, because you're aiming for something greater, something exceptional, and I will show you how to get there.

This book is really about two things:

1. Mastering the art of *counterintuitive thinking*, so you live your best life, pursue your dreams, and can teach others to do the same.

2. Giving great ideas the chance to survive so they can be realized, because this is what pushes humanity forward.

These two goals, you'll see, are deeply connected. They also both rely on your ability to think differently.

If you take this book seriously, it will inspire you to pursue the dreams and ideas burning inside you. It will also strengthen your ability to turn great ideas into tangible realities. Over time, your ideas will grow, leading you to create remarkable things that solve problems for people who desperately need your solution. Perhaps for millions, even billions, of people.

If you're already an entrepreneur, pay close attention. There's a tremendous amount of untapped entrepreneurial potential in the world. Out of the approximately 582 million entrepreneurs globally many are brilliant, dedicated individuals who are not thinking big enough. While you may be generating profits on a small scale, imagine the wealth and impact you could create by tackling large, global challenges. Addressing these challenges not only has the potential to significantly improve the world but, in the process, make you millions to billions. So, this book is also a call to urge every entrepreneur to think bigger—*much* bigger—and consider solutions to problems on a global scale, from eradicating poverty to global access to energy, to making humanity a space civilization.

If that sounds intimidating, don't worry, you'll soon see it's simpler than you think. In fact, it's often easier to pursue big ideas than smaller ones (a principle explored later in this book). Once you learn to think counterintuitively—to question assumptions, explore new perspectives, and seek diverse knowledge to uncover patterns— achieving any goal, big or small, becomes far more attainable.

All you need to get the results you want is this book and an open mind. If you're willing to learn and apply the principles it contains, I promise you'll gain the tools to achieve any dream you desire and become a counterintuitive thinker in the process.

What you'll find in these pages

Counterintuitive thinking is a complex topic, and in this book I've broken it down into two main themes.

First, in Part One, you'll discover why counterintuitive thinking isn't just *valuable* in the pursuit of an extraordinary life, it's *essential*. You will also see how it is a prerequisite for success, especially in our fast-paced, technology-driven, and rapidly evolving future.

Along the way, I'll share a bit of my own story, giving you insight into why I developed a knack for the skill, how it has shaped my perspective and allowed me to achieve many successes. Part One establishes the conceptual framework you need to embrace the counterintuitive principles in Part Two.

Then in Part Two, I share the counterintuitive principles that have shaped my success in business, life, and relationships. They are success-proven, unconventional ideas designed to make you pause, question, and rethink the way you set goals and approach life.

These principles have brought me extraordinary results, and I've watched others achieve the unimaginable by applying them too. Each chapter stands on its own, offering a powerful shift in perspective to a key area of life. Collectively they can redefine how you live, lead, and create.

Whether you're chasing a personal dream, building a business, or simply seeking a better way to navigate life's challenges, these are the principles that will take you from idea to execution and beyond.

Why I wrote this book

Most people don't have a framework for how to make their dreams happen, especially when those dreams are big and bold. Beyond that, practical challenges like finding resources, building support, and overcoming fear make it all too easy to talk ourselves out of taking action. As a result, every day, great ideas that could profoundly benefit humanity die before they have a chance to flourish.

But it doesn't have to be this way. I envision a world where anyone can be the next Albert Einstein (or pick any person you admire). I wrote this book to play my part in making that future happen.

Counterintuitive is also somewhat of a legacy project for me. It is my way to give back. I've learned so much from others who generously shared their knowledge with me, and this is my way of passing it on. In these pages, I'll share what I've learned about entrepreneurship, life, leadership, and relationships in the hope that it will help you create remarkable things for yourself, the world, and the next generation.

There have been many mentors behind my success, but there's one who stands out. Years ago, a man named Jay encouraged me to stay in the U.S. (more on that story later). His generosity and belief in me changed the trajectory of my life. Because of him, I dedicated my life to sharing what I've learned about entrepreneurship and success with others. This book is also my way of honoring him, a man *taught me an invaluable lesson about the power of belief and asked for nothing in return.*

So, with this book I ask for nothing in return but that you *apply what you learn*. And I also want you to know that I believe in you whether we know each other yet or not. Every human is capable of achieving the extraordinary and making the impossible a reality.

In these pages, I share principles that have worked for me and for others. They are time-tested and practical. Use them to turn your ideas and dreams into realities. Apply what you learn and, over time, your success and your confidence will grow. You'll find that this way of living is contagious. You'll inspire others, bring more great ideas to the world, and, as a consequence, make the world a better place. I encourage you to practice and question what you learn here, because questioning is the foundation of counterintuitive thinking.

You should also know that this book is not a traditional 'how-to,' nor is it a business autobiography. It's a series of counterintuitive principles that work on their own and together create a roadmap that leads to the creation of an extraordinary, impactful, and enjoyable life. Along the way, I demonstrate the power of these principles using real-life examples of how I have applied them.

Today, I mentor others because of what I've achieved in business and in life, and I've observed that the greatest obstacle to success isn't resources or talent. It's a lack of intellectual curiosity. To achieve new results, you have to ask new questions. And in a world where technology is replacing skill-based jobs, fresh thinking is more critical than ever.

By the end of this book, if you feel empowered, intrigued, and captivated by the counterintuitive nature of life—and understand how to use this way of thinking to your advantage—then I've done my job. My goal is for you to close this book with the answers you need to succeed in whatever you set out to accomplish. By that point, you'll understand that *counterintuitive* thinking isn't just helpful—it's the only way to make that happen.

Now about that cup of tea…

DEFINING COUNTERINTUITIVE THINKING FOR SUCCESS

CHAPTER 1

COUNTERINTUITIVE THINKING, A PREREQUISITE FOR SUCCESS

"Imagination is more important than knowledge. Knowledge is limited. Imagination encircles the world."

—Albert Einstein

L ET'S START WITH a question: What defines a successful person?

Intuitive thinking might tell us that a successful person is someone with a lot of money, fame, or power. Those status traits are often associated with success, but they don't capture it entirely. So let's begin as we mean to go on by offering a counterintuitive definition:

Success is not measured by the number of digits in your bank account but by the number of lives you improve.

A successful person is someone who pursues their dreams, makes them happen, and does it at scale, helping millions or billions of people live better lives. They pursue their purpose as if it's an obsession, where abundance, fame, and power are natural byproducts they achieve. As a consequence, they also achieve personal fulfillment.

As an exercise to illustrate my point, let's take two very different people: Steve Jobs and Mother Teresa. Regardless of your opinions on these figures, or whether you carry an iPhone or align with Mother Teresa's beliefs, most would agree that they led impactful, massively successful lives. They are revered and admired, and lived the kind of lives many would like to emulate.

So, what commonalities do they share that led society to agree they achieved unprecedented levels of success? It may at first seem that the differences are more striking. Steve Jobs built Apple into a multi-billion-dollar technology company. He brought world-changing computers and mobile devices to market that connected billions of people to each other and gave them access to information that made their lives better. He was wealthy, famous, and powerful among his peers. He was very different from Mother Teresa, who devoted her life to serving the poor and, unlike Jobs, was not particularly concerned with accumulating wealth. Hers was a quiet power and a humble fame.

But like many whose lives are celebrated as 'well-lived,' both of these individuals were driven by an obsession to achieve particular dreams that mattered deeply to them, and they worked tirelessly to make those dreams realities. Over time, they refined their ability to bring their dreams to life and expand upon them. As a result, they improved lives on a massive scale and made a meaningful impact on a large group of people. They may also have achieved some combination of personal fulfilment, financial abundance, accolades, and fame, but these were not their goals, they were merely natural byproducts of their purpose-driven efforts.

If we look at the people of this caliber who came before us, they teach us that true success is about living out our dreams and improving lives. It's about being someone who *creates* and leads. It is about being someone who makes ideas happen and turns them into the products, services, and initiatives that help many people live better lives, making a positive difference for humanity.

You will not be surprised to learn that both Steve Jobs and Mother Teresa were also counterintuitive thinkers. This is because it is not possible to create anything extraordinary if you don't think differently.

Look at any successful person, and you'll see they approach the world differently. They view it through a unique lens, and as a result take bold, innovative actions. That's why the world takes notice of them. They step outside the norm and produce remarkable outcomes.

It's a path I understand because I've experienced it. Counterintuitive thinking is the most critical skill I've used to build an extraordinary life that society recognizes as a successful one.

My counterintuitive journey

I came to the United States with just $5 in my pocket, and built a career in which I've launched and led several billion-dollar and multi-million-dollar companies in vastly different industries. They include an early internet company called InfoSpace that achieved massive success in the days of Web 1.0. Then there's Moon Express, which was the first private company permitted to land on the Moon and has a mission to eventually conduct mining on its surface. And these days my focus is Viome, my latest venture, which is at the forefront of precision health and longevity—our mission is to make aging and illness optional.

These business achievements are why I am called to give advice on stages and in podcasts. People often ask me, *How did you do it?* And what seems to intrigue them even more is that I've done it without sacrificing my relationships. I've been married to my wife, Anu, for over 35 years—she's my best friend—and our children have built businesses that improve millions of lives and are always in the media.

And since my latest venture, Viome, is revolutionizing health and longevity, I too have transformed my health. As I write this, I'm 65 years old with the biological age of 33. Perhaps what's most miraculous is that I love my life, which you'll have to take my word for—a rare combination of success and fulfillment that too few people achieve.

But as you'll see in this book, I am no different from you. Anyone can be a counterintuitive thinker. It's a matter of principles and practice. All of these ventures, and this life, came from being counterintuitive.

Becoming a counterintuitive thinker wasn't something I set out to do. It's a skill I stumbled into. It is a gift that revealed itself through necessity. No one mentored me to think differently or take risks that others might see as foolish. For me, it wasn't a matter of choice but of survival.

Before we dive into why counterintuitive thinking underpins success and how you can use it, I'll share a bit of my backstory, because I realize some people may need to be convinced of the power of this skill.

You have probably heard stories like mine before. It's the classic immigrant story: I grew up with nothing but my loving family, and I came to America with $5 in my pocket. (I really did.) I don't recommend you copy my method: come from nothing. Suffer. Struggle. Work hard. Build a handful of billion-dollar companies. No, that's not the trick to becoming counterintuitive and it's not a requirement.

But I tell you this to illustrate a point: if an immigrant arriving in America with just $5 can build a billion-dollar business and dream of going to the moon, then there's no limit to what *you* can achieve.

I also must preface this story by telling you not to draw unhelpful comparisons. I've seen people do this before. They compare their experience with mine. They look at my journey and say, "That's how he achieved X," where X is something they believe is out of their reach. These perceived differences become their (bogus) reasons why they haven't achieved what they want. So don't let that be you when you read my story or anyone else's.

Plus, keep in mind that a person's beliefs don't form from a single defining moment, but through a series of insights over time. Success works the same way—it's rarely the result of one pivotal event. Yet, when people share their achievements, they often simplify their journey into a neat and tidy formula. Hindsight can distort history, making things seem simpler than they really were. So when others try to follow a successful person's formula for success, in an effort to get similar results, it doesn't work. Life doesn't work that way. Any given success is a result of timing, circumstances, the individual, and their approach.

I share my story here, in part, for those who need evidence of my authority on this subject before taking this book seriously. I also share it for those who underestimate the power of their own minds and need a real example of what becomes possible when counterintuitive thinking is applied.

You'll see that there was a time in my early life when my environment forced me to think differently from everyone around me just to get ahead, using whatever I had, which wasn't much. I did, however, possess one extraordinary asset that shaped my future: my imagination.

Counterintuitive thinking is *fueled* by imagination. Without it, little is possible. And *with* imagination, anything is possible. So with that, let's start where I first learned that counterintuitive thinking is the key to success.

Thinking differently is your access to the life you want

I was born into a family from a remote and rural area in northern India, near the border with Nepal, in a place called Uttar Pradesh. This state is best known as the home of the Taj Mahal, a breathtaking monument often described as a vision of heaven. Its gardens, inspired by Quranic depictions of paradise, feature flowing water and lush greenery, symbolizing eternal peace.

While I grew up in a home with loving parents, my brother and sister and I didn't have much else. We may have lived only a few hundred miles or so from that so-called heaven, but we were raised in a place that some people might consider a hell.

Uttar Pradesh is India's most populous state and one of the poorer regions of the country. Today about 22% of the population is considered multi-dimensionally poor (poor in income, health, education, and living standards). In the 1960s, when I grew up there, it was much higher.

Even today, the modern-day surroundings of the Taj Mahal suffer from severe pollution and overcrowding. The Yamuna River beside it is heavily polluted, and the air quality in the nearby city of Agra is among the worst in India.

At the time, we didn't always have food on the table or a safe place to sleep at night. Many of my childhood memories are faint and fleeting because we were always moving. My father had to transfer frequently because he refused to take bribes—which most government workers like him were expected to do at the time. His transfers were always to remote areas that were very poor and under-resourced. At schools in those places, my fellow students and I learned sitting on a dirt floor.

My father was a civil engineer and building inspector. In the 1960s and 1970s, as is the case now, working as a civil engineer was not a bad job. It would generally guarantee a person a life of moderate affluence and firm entrenchment in the middle class. My dad's job was to go to construction sites and ensure developers were building safely, not cutting corners to turn quick profits. But, since corruption ruled much of India's economy and public sector at that time, it was expected that building inspectors and civil engineers working for the government would 'supplement' their income with a steady stream of bribes.

Most people doing the same work as my father made 10% of their earnings in salary. The other 90% came from kickbacks. It was a pyramid-like structure. Lower-level civil servants accepted bribes from building contractors and kept a small percentage for themselves. The rest was sent up the hierarchical government chain to local managers, who took their cut and passed on an even bigger percentage to regional managers and politicians. This scheme reached the top of the bureaucracy.

My father believed his job was to ensure the safety of every building he approved. He felt personally responsible for any accidents that might occur as a result of his decisions. If he accepted kickbacks and signed off on shoddy work, he would have shared the blame for any lives lost or people injured. In his industry, many were willing to risk serious harm to others just to make money—builders, bureaucrats, and contractors alike. But my father always said, "There are some things you can't put a price on."

And so, he declined all bribes. He chose his conscience and honesty over significant additional income from the corrupt payment scheme. As a result, our family struggled financially and life was extremely difficult for us.

Young and arrogant, for many years I blamed my dad for our poverty. I didn't realize that he was teaching me one of the most valuable lessons anyone could ever learn. It was a lesson about honesty, self-reliance, and self-respect, all of which have helped me immensely in business and life. And later, when I became a father myself, I saw his world from a new perspective. To be the head of a household and for there to be even one day when you cannot put food in front of your family must have been terrible.

But having nothing was the beginning of my understanding that, in actuality, I had *everything*. And, I assure you, you have everything you need, too.

I had this magical mind and complete power over it. I could expand it. I could use it to learn skills for a better life. I could use it to think differently, which helped me to be more resourceful and to get what I wanted and to make my dreams happen. My mother also reinforced this belief in me. She knew the only way her kids could escape poverty was by using their minds to learn. Education was the path forward. She would say, "Son, you can do anything you want. The sky's the limit." Said differently, she was telling me that with your mind you have all you need to free yourself from all the perceived limits in life.

Your mind is all you need to see the world from a different perspective and to learn skills and grow. This was all I had. And as it turned out, it *was* all I needed.

Over the years, I've harnessed the power of my mind to achieve things I once never dared to imagine. The first of these impossible feats was to win scholarships—a guaranteed escape to a better future.

That realization hit me with overwhelming clarity one night when I was just ten years old. My father was in the throes of a major crisis, and in that moment, it became painfully clear: I, alone with my mind, was the key to rewriting my story.

Although no one in our household had any illusions of wealth, my father never let us know how poor we were. He was a very calm and measured man who always wore a smile, no matter how much adversity we faced. But on this one night he came home panicked.

He had been seriously threatened by those who expected him to collect bribes and share them up the bureaucratic chain. He worried that he would leave our home one day, and something bad would happen to him—that he would never return. My mother asked him if there was any way the government could get him a bodyguard.

He called me and my two siblings to the family table and then he rifled through a small pouch, pulled out a cluster of rupees and spread them out. It was the equivalent of around $50 today. "This is your inheritance," he said, looking each of us in the eye. We could tell that he was deadly serious. "If something should ever happen to me, this is all the money I can give you to build your lives." He told us to split it into three. "Go and become something on your own," he urged.

Looking back, that moment shaped who I am today. It was when I truly became an entrepreneur. I realized I was responsible for my path. My father had spent his life teaching me the value of honesty, but in that moment, I understood what fueled it: the importance of self-reliance. If I wanted to succeed, I'd have to take charge and make it happen myself.

The turning point

When you're poor, all you can think about is money, but today, now that I have enough to live on, I know that no amount of money from my father could have made me successful. Even if he had given me $100 million, it would have simply made me rich and likely complacent. The money on the table in front of my father wasn't my inheritance; my inheritance came in the form of my father's lessons.

From that point on, I realized I would have to do everything and anything I could to earn scholarships so I could attend school. It was up to me and my trusty mind—and its powers to think, learn, and imagine—to make it happen. I became a learning, studying machine.

Thankfully my hard work paid off. In 1982, I went to the Indian Institute of Technology (IIT) on a full scholarship (which was the toughest school to get admission to) and earned an undergraduate degree as an industrial engineer. Then I earned my graduate degree in personnel management from Xavier School of Management (XLRI) and eventually, earned myself a U.S. work visa, a magic golden ticket to my future.

Landing in the U.S. was incredible. I had a fresh start. I had hope. But the elation didn't last. My first years were very tough, and, once again, my imagination saved me. I was the only brown person in a town of 100 people and I felt I didn't belong. In these first years, I suffered many hardships, but what I learned yet again is that my greatest asset is my mind. It's what got me through. I used my thinking powers to be resourceful and to get what I wanted no matter what obstacles were in front of me. My mind always helped me turn barriers into opportunities.

Eventually, the skills of counterintuitive thinking that I was building helped me find my first job, and then that led to Silicon Valley and an even better role at Microsoft. Thanks to my counterintuitive thinking I excelled there. This gave me the confidence to eventually launch my own business, which became a $40bn early internet success.

Through it all, my mind helped me navigate every hardship that came my way. As we move through this book, I'll share more stories to demonstrate the power of the counterintuitive principles I teach you here. But for now, I ask you to consider this idea, which became a core belief of mine early on and has been reinforced throughout my life: when you can see things differently, you're never stuck—there is always a way to achieve what you want.

My journey taught me that my dreams were mine alone. The same is true for you: your dreams are yours and no one can take them away from you. Dream so big that people think you're crazy. And then pursue those dreams, because with a curious mind, you have everything it takes to make them a reality.

You don't need to have had an upbringing like mine to succeed. You can start right here, right now, with whatever backstory you have. All it takes is an open mind—just enough to explore what it truly means to think counterintuitively. By doing so, you'll unlock the power of this skill and discover how it can be your gateway to the business and life you desire.

The most important question

Enough about me, let's get back to you and why you're here. It's time for me to give you what my dad gave me when he presented me with that fistful of rupees: self-reliance and the understanding that within you—with your ability to think and take action—you have everything you need to get the life you want.

First, I want you to ask yourself one of life's most important questions:

When you wake up, are you excited to jump out of bed?

I ask this because there is a critical rule that I live by and share with others. I always say, "If you wake up in the morning and are not excited to jump out of the bed, quit what you're doing and go do something that matters to you."

So consider whether you are stepping into a day and a life that truly excites you each morning. Do you feel inspired and grateful for the life you're living? Or do you wake up dreading your work, begrudgingly rolling out of bed, and trudging to the kitchen with a sense of despair for the day ahead?

Perhaps your days feel just 'okay.' Maybe you're living a life that's 'pretty good,' with the vague hope that it will be better someday, but without any real plan to make it happen.

Does this question make you feel a little uneasy? Do you find yourself wanting to avoid it, even though you're the only one here, quietly contemplating it while reading this book? If so, that's a clear sign it's time for a change.

Imagine if you quit what you're doing now and pursued something that truly excites you. Just by seriously considering this, you have already taken the first step towards a life of abundance. But here's the reality: most people won't take this step. They tell themselves they'll do it someday, but not today. Others might dismiss the idea entirely, thinking, "That's easy for you to say, Naveen—you have all the resources you need!" Or they might think I'm completely nuts and impractical. But it's precisely this mentality that keeps the cycle going. And who does it hurt in the end? Only you.

Before putting counterintuitive thinking into practice, you must first consider what you want. You must define what success looks like *for you*. What will get you excited to jump out of bed in the morning? You will only care about the *how* if you define your *why*—the thing you are pursuing.

Keep this in your mind as we continue our journey. Begin to ponder what matters to you and keep piecing it together. Next, we'll delve deeper into the science and art of what it means to be counterintuitive, so you *really* understand where I'm taking you.

CHAPTER 2

WHAT IT MEANS TO BE COUNTERINTUITIVE, AND WHY IT'S EFFECTIVE

"Don't be too quick to accept the way things are being done. Question whether there's a better way. Very often you will find that once you make this break from the usual way—and incidentally, this is probably the hardest thing to do—and start on a new track your horizon of new thoughts immediately broadens."

—Nathaniel J. Wyeth, American inventor and businessman

SINCE WE'RE GOING to explore how to be a counterintuitive thinker extensively in this book, it will be useful to define what it means to be *counterintuitive*.

Being counterintuitive means thinking and doing things differently than what common sense or initial instinct might suggest. A counterintuitive action might feel illogical yet, as we will learn, lead to better results. Perhaps surprisingly, thinking counterintuitively and taking counterintuitive actions can also make getting what you want simpler. This is because when you think and act counterintuitively, you will see that you often work with, rather than against, human nature and the way the world works.

The best way to grasp the power of counterintuitive thinking is with some common scenarios most of us have experienced. Let's start with the example of a salesperson attempting to give you the 'hard sell.' Their approach is based on the common misconception that the more energy you put into your sales pitch, the more effective it will be.

If you have been the target of pushy salespeople, you get how their approach makes you not want to buy. In reality, though it seems counterintuitive, if you're in sales you tend to sell more when you are less pushy, listen more, and share authentically about yourself and why what you're selling matters to you. The best way to connect is not on an intellectual level, it is through emotion and shared experience or struggle. And this is why I always say I am a businessman who never sells. I avoid it at all costs, and that is why I sell so well!

This is the counterintuitive principle 'you will sell more if you sell less.'

People buy from you when they believe in you. They align with your value system and your *why*, your reason to do what you are doing. This is what builds trust between people. Sales is not about selling your product but about building relationships and trust.

Instead of selling, I take on problems and missions that matter to me and then I share why they matter.

For instance, when I talk about my current company, Viome, I often share how my dad died from cancer and the impact it had on my life. It means a lot to me to solve the problem of chronic disease and aging. I realized the pain and suffering we endure as we age is unnecessary. Technology can help us not only to minimize encroaching decrepitude, but it can even help to reverse aging and to stay vital.

My story demonstrates that I am not in this business solely for money. Caring—and not selling—is the best way to sell. When you believe in your cause, you should never have to *sell* anything to anyone. If you do, it's a sign that you are in the wrong line of work, and this is true whether you run a business or work for one.

Another more obvious counterintuitive principle that most have experienced is, 'go slow to go fast.' Common sense tells us that the more speed you employ, the faster you go, but you can't be a great driver if you don't first learn very slowly how to turn a wheel, check your blind spots, parallel park, and use the brakes. You must be able to break a skill down and learn it piece by piece to be able to do it with ease. This principle is true in driving but also in learning pretty much anything. It's actually what we're doing right now. We're breaking down what it means to be counterintuitive so you see the value of the principles taught later in the book and will be more likely to use them.

Even when it comes to writing a book like this one, there is a counterintuitive approach to get it done faster. Rather than sitting for endless hours pushing through writer's block, 'plan more, dictate more, write less.' This is how counterintuitive thinkers can create and finish a book in half the time. Spending less time writing a book might help you get it done faster, which may seem quite paradoxical.

The deeper you dive into this topic, the more you will find that the most effective approaches to getting what you want in any area of life are counterintuitive. Here is a short list of another ten counterintuitive truths that you may well recognize, and that have been shared over the years by scientists, philosophers, and thought leaders new and old.

Ten common examples of counterintuitive thinking in practice

1. The harder you try to impress someone, the less likely they feel drawn to you.

2. The best way to meet your soulmate is to learn to love being on your own.

3. The only certainty in life is change.

4. The more choices you have, the harder it is to make a choice.

5. If you admit your shortcomings and vulnerabilities, people are more likely to think you are courageous, trustworthy, and powerful.

6. The more you learn about a topic, the less you realize you know.

7. The crazier your ideas, the more people think you're brilliant.

8. The more failures you learn from, the more likely you are to succeed.

9. The less safe you feel, the more likely you are to have options and lifelong security.

10. If you feel ashamed, the best thing to do is practice courage by being honest with yourself and others about it.

There are hundreds to thousands of these principles you can find with a simple internet search (or perhaps from your personal experience) to prove the power of being counterintuitive.

Counterintuitive thinking is effective because *life itself is innately counterintuitive.* While we use logic to make progress in life, humans are not logical or predictable at their core. We are driven by emotions. The world itself is illogical too, even though we don't like to acknowledge this. While we look for patterns in areas like the weather, in reality these forces are totally out of our control. From the perspective of our limited understanding, the world is ultimately illogical, complex, and constantly shifting.

But this doesn't mean that counterintuitive thinking is all spontaneous chaos. It is helpful to understand that there are scientific and artistic components to it. There are empirical principles about the nature of reality that show why counterintuitive actions and behaviors are effective, smart, and logical. And alongside the science there is art and beauty in its practice.

Let's first look at the science, so you see what I am saying is not solely conjecture.

The *science* of counterintuitive thinking

There are five fascinating scientific principles that show how the world and life itself is counterintuitive and why an 'illogical' approach can lead to very logical and remarkable outcomes. This is for anyone that needs scientific proof of why being counterintuitive is smart (and also because there are times where you might need a reminder).

Principle 1: Causes can have delayed effects

In science, this is known as *time-lagged causality*—the idea that an action taken at one moment can produce its most meaningful results long after the action itself, and often in an entirely different context. In complex systems, causes and effects are rarely immediate. They unfold over time, accumulate quietly, and surface only when conditions are right.

Consider that the full impact of something happening today may not be felt for months or even years, and when it does appear, it may show up somewhere you never expected.

For instance, while you are reading this book now, it could be five years before you find yourself working on a project where a single idea from these pages suddenly becomes the key that unlocks an extraordinary result. The cause occurred long ago; the effect arrives precisely when it is needed.

This is why actions that seem 'not useful' in the present—such as learning a skill you don't yet see a practical application for—can be among the smartest investments you make. Science shows that knowledge, experience, and relationships often operate through accumulation and delayed payoff, not immediate reward.

Perhaps it's time to pick up the ukulele, read a financial education book on your lunch break, or have a conversation with someone you might otherwise dismiss as a waste of time. Any one of these actions could become the missing piece that solves a problem six months from now—or changes the trajectory of your life years down the line.

Principle 2: Cause and effect are often interchangeable

In many real-world systems, cause and effect are not linear but circular. Science describes this as a *feedback loop*, where an effect feeds back into the system and becomes a new cause, reinforcing and amplifying what came before.

Success in any area—be it your career, academics, or personal life—can spark a cycle that reinforces itself and leads to success in another area.

For example, imagine being awarded 'Employee of the Month' by your boss. You leave work feeling proud, and on your subway ride home, instead of avoiding eye contact with strangers, you smile at an attractive person across the aisle. A conversation sparks and leads to a date and, eventually, marriage. This relationship further boosts your confidence. It motivates you to set bigger career goals. You decide you no longer want to be a salesperson; you want to run the department. With hard work and determination, you move into management and eventually the C-suite.

What's happening here is that the original 'effect'—a boost in confidence—quickly becomes the cause of future outcomes. Each result feeds back into the system, creating momentum.

This is also why when you build positive skills in one area, they naturally impact other areas. It is why focusing on strengthening your body and attaining superior health so often leads to better performance at work. In feedback-driven systems, progress compounds because cause and effect continuously trade places.

Principle 3: One event can have multiple outcomes

In complex systems, a single cause rarely produces a single, predictable effect. Science refers to this as *nonlinearity* and *emergence*—the idea that one event can branch into multiple outcomes, many of which could not have been anticipated at the outset.

It is not possible for anyone to ever truly forecast or anticipate the full impact of a single action, behavior, or achievement.

The internet is a powerful example of this. Initially, its primary effect was communication. It was developed as a tool for researchers and academics to exchange information quickly and efficiently, and this was considered the most important benefit at the time. Over the years, however, other effects of the internet proved to be far more significant.

E-commerce emerged as a revolutionary new way to conduct business, reshaping entire industries and altering how value is created and exchanged. Social media platforms evolved and now play a major role in shaping public discourse, connecting people globally, and influencing culture and politics—outcomes that were never part of the original design brief.

This is why what appears to be a relatively minor action can trigger a cascade of unexpected and often positive outcomes. In *nonlinear* systems, the real impact of an event is rarely limited to its original intention.

Principle 4: Motivations can change while the outcomes stay the same

In complex systems, the *drivers* of behavior can shift without altering the ultimate result. Science describes this as *equifinality*—the idea that the same outcome can be reached through different motivations, paths, or internal states over time.

When I started my first company, my primary focus was on innovation, customer experience, and creating more value for others. Yet the ultimate outcome was tremendous financial, emotional, spiritual, and intellectual success. I now understand that making money is simply a byproduct of doing things that improve other people's lives (more on this to come).

That financial success could have led me to retire. Instead, the profound fulfillment I experienced deepened my understanding of what life and business are really about. As a result, even in my 60s, I now work 16 hours a day, seven days a week, focused on solving larger societal problems.

Any process you start—whether it's a business, a relationship, or a personal goal—can continue evolving as your motivations and circumstances change. What matters is not clinging to the original reason you began, but adapting to the new forces that sustain momentum and fuel growth (we'll explore this deeply in Chapter 7).

This is why an action that seems mundane—or even slightly risky—today can lead to massive success later. In systems governed by *equifinality*, the destination can remain constant even as your reasons for continuing evolve, making long-term commitment not only rational, but essential.

Principle 5: Quick wins can become long-term losses, and vice versa

Any action has both short-term and long-term consequences, and we might take action expecting one result but getting a very different outcome in the end. Something that seems good in the short term can have a negative impact later. The reverse is also true.

Spinach is generally considered healthy, but it is also very high in oxalates. In many people, limited gut microbial capacity to break down oxalates can increase oxalate absorption and the risk of kidney stone formation. For these individuals, consuming large amounts of high-oxalate foods such as spinach and almonds every day may not be ideal. Sometimes the counterintuitive action of not eating the spinach, when everyone else is telling you to do it, is better for you!

One aspect of counterintuitive thinking is to consider the long-term impacts of an action. While we saw in principle three that it's not possible to foresee all outcomes, if you take the time to map out the logical likelihoods, you will be as prepared as possible for the longer term. When you think this way an idea that seems good now might actually be a very bad idea, or vice versa.

With these five scientific principles that underpin the nature of reality and how the world works, you can already see that counterintuitive thinking can sometimes feel like you're going against the grain and take you out of your comfort zone. It can be tempting to avoid counterintuitive behavior because our brains like order and safety. This is why taking counterintuitive action can feel unnatural, illogical, or wrong—even when it's not.

Knowing the science of why counterintuitive thinking and action is effective will help you get better at looking at the counterintuitive world and working with the information you have in smart ways. This in turn enables you to make the most informed decisions and get more of what you want. But to be a *really* effective counterintuitive thinker, you also need to see it as an art form. The art comes down to knowing and emulating five core counterintuitive traits, then using them strategically in combination with the science.

The *art* of counterintuitive thinking

As I've connected the dots on my own actions, through research and from observing the most successful counterintuitive people I know, I have learned they possess five key traits, and they are remarkably similar to traits that artistic and creative people tend to hold.

Let's briefly touch on each of these artistic counterintuitive traits because, by the end of this book, if I have done my job, you can expect to be someone who possesses them. You might even do an impromptu audit on yourself now. As you read each trait, ask yourself: to what extent does this apply to me?

Trait 1: Question everything, always

Counterintuitive thinkers instinctively challenge accepted beliefs. They're the kind of people who, when told, "This is how it's always been done," respond with "why?" This pursuit of deeper understanding helps them find unconventional solutions that others might miss. They are the kind of person that questions why pizza boxes are square, why elevators don't move sideways, and why cheese is white or yellow, not magenta.

This trait also helps explain why non-experts are better at disruption than experts. Once you become an expert, you tend to approach change in your field in terms of incremental improvements and not wholesale disruption. This is why I've succeeded with companies in industries I know nothing about!

Counterintuitive thinkers remain flexible and open to different viewpoints. This trait allows them to adapt to new information, embrace unconventional ideas, and pivot when necessary. By being open-minded, they can synthesize diverse perspectives into well-rounded solutions that others might overlook.

Trait 2: Explore situations from different perspectives

For counterintuitive thinkers, approaching challenges from one angle is like playing a piano with only one key, which makes no sense. They are people who treat problems in life like an improv show, where anything and everything is fair game to change and shift. Whether upside-down, inside-out, or sideways, they'll explore every approach, no matter how outlandish it might seem at first.

This constant juggling of perspectives makes them creative powerhouses and nimble adapters, ready to pivot in the moment a roadblock appears. They also revel in complexity, weaving together opposing ideas to find innovative solutions. They do not see life as black and white. It's zebra-striped, with a hint of neon pink. By embracing conflicting concepts, they find answers where others see dead ends.

Legendary physicist Albert Einstein was good at this. His paradoxical idea that light behaves both as a wave and a particle allowed him to bridge the gap between classical and quantum physics, forever changing how we perceive energy and matter.

Trait 3: Identify patterns and strategically decide whether to harness or avoid them

People who are counterintuitive are calculated risk takers. They excel at pattern recognition with a twist, interpreting trends and signals differently, identifying opportunities hidden beneath surface data. Together, these components allow counterintuitive thinkers to challenge the status quo, discover innovative solutions, and drive progress where conventional methods fall short.

This is why they're the kind of people that offer fresh insights that reshape how problems are approached and solved.

Later in this book, I'll share a story about how I did this, and how it led to success with my first internet company. For now, to illustrate the effectiveness of this trait, I will tell you that while everyone wanted to create the next big internet business, I wanted to create the unsexy business the big internet businesses needed. I saw a trend and I used it strategically to be different. I became the business everyone needed and was far more successful.

Trait 4: Leverage imagination to uncover what doesn't exist, but should

Imagination is key for counterintuitive thinkers because they see beyond what currently exists and envision what *could* be. They push boundaries and think outside the box, leading to ideas that seem improbable until they are realized. Their ability to use their imagination results in breakthroughs that redefine industries or create new ones.

Walt Disney famously said, "If you can dream it, you can do it." He used his imagination to create Disneyland, a theme park that brought fairy tales and adventure to life. At a time when amusement parks were simple, he envisioned a fully immersive experience that became a blueprint for future entertainment venues.

Trait 5: Demonstrate courage

It might be tempting to think that counterintuitive thinkers are fearless. And it may even appear like they operate without fear. Yet, experiencing fear is innately part of being human. Counterintuitive thinkers are not fearless, but courageous.

It takes something to challenge the status quo and to choose to be unconventional in a world where we are all trained to conform from pre-school onward. As a counterintuitive thinker, you will still experience nerves. You may also have to contend with institutional thinkers that lash out when you introduce new and disruptive ideas. Your intellect will be challenged and you may find yourself in a fight to overcome the inertia of the ordinary. This will take courage. In fact, courage is critical. And we will cover in depth how to be resilient in Chapter 7.

However, courage gets easier with the recognition that counterintuitive thinking is not just a way to get smarter and improve at life—it's the only route to becoming massively successful at anything. If you're not willing to challenge the obvious and rethink everything, you're holding yourself back from the success you desire.

Breakthrough results start with counterintuitive thoughts

To achieve an extraordinary life, you must choose a different route than most people. This is especially true if you want to be an innovator in business or a respected leader in a field. You can't simply do what's obvious, because the obvious is what most people are doing. In other words, *to be extraordinary you have to think outside the ordinary.*

If you do what others do, you can only expect similar outcomes, which only ever lead to average results. While doing what everyone else does is comfortable and safe, it limits you to a life of moderate success. Rarely does anyone look at someone who has merely met common expectations and think, *Wow, they're exceptionally successful.*

Now, what's also funny is that when you ask people about their life goals, most express a desire to stand out—to accomplish something remarkable or unique. Deep down, many believe that life's purpose is to leave the world better than they found it. Yet, ironically, many still choose to conform and play it safe, doing what everyone else does. How does that align with their deeper aspirations? How does that make sense?

And so, if the ultimate goal of this book is to help you achieve success by being a counterintuitive thinker, along with the happiness and satisfaction that result, we need to think counterintuitively about happiness itself. So, let's talk about what it means to live a happy life through a counterintuitive lens.

CHAPTER 3

HAPPINESS, A REDEFINITION WITH A COUNTERINTUITIVE SPIN

"Success is not the key to happiness. Happiness is the key to success. If you love what you are doing, you will be successful."

—Albert Schweitzer, German polymath

IN WESTERN SOCIETY, there is a common idea that we will be happy once we achieve some goal we envision for ourselves. Once we have enough money to buy a house or afford a sports car, or when we meet the right person, everything will be perfect. We will have achieved 'success' and that will 'make us happy.' But, when we pursue outcomes we believe will make us happy, what are we truly after? The answer is that we're seeking these achievements in order *to feel* a certain way. The accolades and possessions we chase represent the freedom, control, and happiness we hope to gain.

When it comes to success, I've learned a counterintuitive approach makes it easier to achieve: *Forget about what you think you want. Focus on improving the lives of other people, in the unique way that personally satisfies you, and everything else will fall into place.*

Improving lives by solving a major problem that impacts a large group of people, in an area that matters to you, is your access to financial and relational abundance, along with the lasting type of happiness we call *fulfillment*. So, improve lives, solve big problems, and the rest is easy to achieve. Everything you need and want happens naturally.

The inverse, focusing on accumulating money, power, status by any means—which is the conventional way to pursue success and happiness, keeps you in a constant state of wanting. It keeps you seeking fulfillment and never getting there. For many people, what they *believe* will bring them success or happiness causes them the opposite.

I once thought this way too, believing a Rolex watch would make me happy. This was when I had very little. I figured if I could one day afford a Rolex, I would have 'made it.' Around the same time, I had a friend who made six figures. He was an engineer who worked for a company that was acquired and he made $100,000 from the acquisition. I thought if one day I could just have $100,000 I would be happy.

When I reached the six-figure mark, I still wasn't happy. I realized that I wouldn't be happy until I made it to a million, and then a million after tax, and then one million after paying for a house. When I had achieved that, I realized I needed $5 million to be happy. Of course, I was chasing the wrong thing. Once I figured that out, I found the greatest happiness in doing things that improve humanity. What about that Rolex? Now that I can easily afford it, I don't want one. I'm happy with my more practical Apple Watch.

The happiness trap

Most people have been conditioned to think that they need someone or something to make them happy. But this thinking gives the remote control of your happiness to other people and things. And they are never the solution they appear to be. It might be a cliché, but happiness really must be found within. If you are unhappy inside, you can be sitting in paradise and will still be unhappy. But if you are *truly* happy at your core, you carry that happiness wherever you go. Most people look for happiness everywhere without ever realizing that it exists somewhere within them.

People also conflate material 'success' with happiness, and so they apply similar thinking. They imagine that some achievement or object will make them successful, when what they're really seeking is a feeling of happiness. This is deeply flawed thinking, but it's easy to fall into, because society is full of messages that reinforce this version of success and happiness—it implies that millionaires are inherently happy and that driving luxury cars and chartering airplanes signifies achievement. It's easy to internalize these messages and adopt them without questioning whether they reflect your own values. But if they don't align with what truly matters to you, achieving them will only ever get you fleeting happiness and won't lead to lasting fulfillment.

Instead, think about your life through the lens of a massive mission that solves a problem for a large number of people. Of course, this line of thinking can be rather counterintuitive, because we are all good at being very self-focused. So, what if you approached life thinking this: *I won't be satisfied until I solve a major problem for a massive number of people.*

Imagine what tackling a massive problem that matters to you every day will do for your quality of life. If you pursue a mission that matters to you, especially if it's a problem you've been impacted by, then even the mere thought of it will energize you. Simply being someone who pursues a massive mission to solve a problem is leading a noble life that others will applaud you for, but, more importantly, it will be a mission and a life that you can feel good about.

Eastern philosophy tends to see more clearly that success is rooted in finding genuine happiness within. It's not about what you have. It's more about *who you are being and what you are doing*. It's about legacy—what you create in the world that makes it better and what you leave behind. From this perspective, even if you don't achieve a goal, simply pushing that goal far enough along for someone else to take it across the finish line is a success you can be proud of.

Now, both Western and Eastern perspectives on happiness have valid elements. There will always be collective ideals of success that are easy to buy into, but it's equally important to recognize the role of personal satisfaction, character, and contributions in guiding your own unique vision of success. Money and material items, like a nice car or home, aren't inherently bad; they often enhance our life experiences. But, ultimately, it's up to each of us to define what happiness really means to us, independent of others' expectations, and do it in the context of an important mission that improves lives.

When you discover a purpose that truly matters to you, you'll never lie in bed wondering why you're waking up. Instead, you'll jump out of bed energized, driven by the sense that what you're doing isn't just a job, but a calling—something deeply meaningful.

So ask yourself a serious question: *What am I willing to die for?* It should feel that important. When you find that purpose, it will give each day—and your whole life—direction.

What purpose could you pursue, even today, that would not only fulfill you but also improve the lives of others? I ask this because it's the backdrop for the life you create, where you will use your counterintuitive thinking skills. And it's the most important question to ask considering the future we're heading into, in which counterintuitive thinking will give you an unbeatable edge. It will no longer be a nice-to-have skill, it will be a necessity. As we near the end of Part One, let's reflect on that thought.

From optional skill to necessity

In a world that is being shaped by exponential, unpredictable change, those who thrive will be the ones who can overcome their brain's natural tendency for linear thinking. Our minds are hardwired for gradual progress. They struggle to keep up with the accelerating pace of technological advancements that now define our reality.

Most people don't think enough about how technology grows faster than we do. Each advancement builds on the last. The doubling of transistor counts on chips every one to two years also continues to make computers faster, smaller, and more powerful.

It's easier to understand the impact of exponential technological growth with an example, so let's think for a moment about cell phones.

Early mobile phones in the 1980s were bulky, expensive devices with limited features. By the early 2000s, advances in miniaturization and processing power brought smaller, affordable phones with texting and basic internet access. Then, in 2007, the iPhone revolutionized the industry, introducing a device that combined computing power, high-quality cameras, and constant connectivity into a single handheld tool. Today, smartphones are ubiquitous—nearly 90% of the global population owns a mobile phone, offering instant communication, limitless information, and an array of personal and professional tools at their fingertips. From 0% to 90% in around 40 years—truly exponential.

If it feels like technology is everywhere, constantly improving, and making the world more advanced and tech-driven, that's because it is. And this trend isn't slowing down.

Now contrast this with our brains, which are still hardwired for linear thinking. Despite all the societal and technological progress, human brain structure has remained largely unchanged for around 300,000 years, since the emergence of modern *Homo sapiens*.

In this rapidly evolving world, those who can't break free from linear thinking will struggle to anticipate disruptions and risk missing valuable opportunities by focusing only on immediate gains. Counterintuitive thinkers, on the other hand, will thrive. They'll embrace change, view challenges from multiple perspectives, and turn a constantly shifting environment into an advantage.

Which do you want to be? It seems rather obvious to me.

By learning how to think differently you will be able to easily adapt to a radically shifting landscape. You'll be better at having foresight, navigating complexity with agility. You will seize opportunities others will overlook. Counterintuitive thinking isn't just about surviving change; it's about excelling in a world that *requires* us to do it.

If you were to consolidate the expert projections from academia and global institutions regarding the top skills to succeed in the future, you might well end up with a list that looks something like this:

1. **Complex problem-solving:** Tackling multifaceted issues and developing actionable solutions across disciplines.

2. **Critical thinking:** Objectively evaluating information to make decisions; analyzing trends and breaking down complex data.

3. **Creativity:** Generating new ideas and adapting quickly to innovation-driven change.

4. **Emotional intelligence:** Managing emotions, empathizing, and enhancing interpersonal connections.

5. **Adaptability:** Embracing change, learning new skills, and shifting roles or industries.

6. **Digital literacy:** Proficiency in tools like coding, AI, data analysis, and cybersecurity.

7. **Leadership:** Inspiring, influencing, and fostering inclusive, collaborative environments.

8. **Collaboration:** Effectively working in diverse, often remote, teams with strong communication skills.

9. **Cognitive flexibility:** Switching between concepts and adapting to new situations.

Counterintuitive thinking is the connective tissue through all of these skills. So picture a future where technology is amplified beyond anything we know today (a likely scenario, given the modern rate of innovation) and these attributes are the ones that will enable you to harness new technologies and thrive. What is possible for you if you're counterintuitive?

Imagine yourself with a counterintuitive edge

Let's fast forward to a future where technology continues to accelerate and shape our world in miraculous ways…

Imagine a world where schools teach kids not only reading and math, but critical skills like adaptability, emotional intelligence, and complex problem-solving—the very tools they'll need to thrive. Picture homes that double as health hubs, equipped with precision health tools that monitor and manage our well-being in real time. Our homes might even detect illness before symptoms appear, alerting us to changes in our health, which we can monitor directly through our personal data networks.

It will no doubt be a world where AI and robots are no longer cutting-edge concepts but integral parts of daily life. You might grab a coffee brewed by a robotic barista in the morning, hop into a self-driving car that takes you safely to your destination, and even work alongside AI systems that enhance your productivity, creativity, and learning. With technology replacing mundane and repetitive labor, governments will be compelled to adopt universal basic income, recognizing that human potential is better spent tackling humanity's biggest challenges.

The opportunities are boundless. We'll see breakthroughs in sustainable living, space exploration, and even the eradication of diseases. But with these advancements comes a new kind of complexity, a future so rapid and multilayered that without a new way of thinking, it could be overwhelming. The people who can embrace this complexity, who can think counterintuitively, will be the ones who navigate this world most effectively, seizing opportunities and shaping the future.

Now imagine that you are a counterintuitive thinker, always prepared, focused on innovating, and completely empowered because you know how to *use your mind creatively*. What will you do? Who will you be? What solutions will you create?

This future is yours if you want it. It simply starts with being willing to embrace the idea that thinking differently is your access to whatever you want. A mind that knows how to question and see situations from multiple perspectives is your insurance policy for life and your path to success. Nothing can stop you because you always know your way through. There is always a solution and anything is possible.

So that's the dream. In Part Two we'll find out how to make it a reality.

PART TWO

COUNTERINTUITIVE PRINCIPLES FOR WINNING AT LIFE AND BUSINESS

CHAPTER 4

COUNTERINTUITIVE MINDSET

"There are no limitations to the mind except those we acknowledge. Both poverty and riches are the offspring of thought."

—Napoleon Hill, author of *Think and Grow Rich*

I N MY SEATTLE home office, there's a glass case that holds what I see as a representation of tangible possibility. Inside is my collection of space rocks—a mix of meteorites and Moon rocks I've gathered over the years. As far as I know, it's the largest private collection, rivaling those in many museums.

One of my favorites is a fragment of the Sylacauga meteorite, even though it injured a woman in Alabama in 1954. This incident was the only recorded instance of a person being struck by a meteorite. Imagine being hit by something that traveled through space! It apparently came crashing through her roof and landed on her where she sat. Fortunately, it only inflicted a large bruise. Another piece in my collection is a shimmering slice of the Seymchan meteorite from Russia, with intricate crystals revealing formations from deep within an asteroid. But the piece with the deepest meaning for me is an ancient rock from the Moon. When I hand a visitor one of these rocks, I hope they feel the same awe I do—a reminder that we're all, in some way, touched by the stars and that, with imagination, anything is possible.

For as long as I can remember, I've been captivated by the Moon and the vast sky it hangs in. During my childhood, my family and I mostly lived in small rural towns, and as I mentioned earlier, we moved often thanks to my father's job. In the darkness of these villages, where there was little light pollution, I'd often gaze up at the night sky, mesmerized by that glowing orb and all the potential it held.

One night, as I looked up, I had a realization: the richest person in the world was seeing this very same Moon. And in my rural village with no light pollution, I might even have the better view! In that moment, I went from feeling small to powerful, seeing myself as part of something vast in which all people were considered equal.

That was around 1969, the year that Neil Armstrong walked on the Moon. I was perhaps nine or ten years old then. Years later, in my early 50s, I founded Moon Express, the first private company authorized to go to the Moon—a project that was, for me, a leap from a life of simple dreams to actively reaching for the stars. (We'll explore more about that adventure in the next chapter.)

So why am I telling you all this Moon stuff? Because, I want to help other people to feel like I did as a child, gazing at the Moon and sensing infinite possibility. A boundless imagination is the greatest tool to overcome our limitations.

For a ten-year-old Indian boy from a struggling family, imagination was the very tool I needed, when I had nothing, yet literally wanted the Moon. It was the one tool I didn't have to earn, or develop, or go to school for. In a way, having nothing freed me to focus on my imagination and what it offered—in the long term it was arguably my greatest advantage in life.

Your limitations can be your greatest assets. They might just be what you need to help you get what you want.

Much as I would love to hand you one of my space rocks and see whether you feel the same inspiration I do, that is not immediately practical. So, let's do the next best thing. You'll need your imagination for this.

Imagine with me: you're outside, looking up at the sky, feeling the cool night air and gazing at a full, glowing Moon. Don't worry too much about the details—it doesn't matter if you conjure up a rural setting or are glancing up at the Moon between skyscrapers in a bustling city. What matters is that you're staring up at the Moon, immersed in the scene you've imagined.

Now consider this: who else is looking at the Moon at this very moment? You're not the only one. Around the world, countless others are gazing up as well. Maybe they're famous figures, or ordinary people living their lives that in the moment glance skyward on the same day as you do.

Whoever they are, they will see the same Moon. You have the same access to the Moon as anyone else. In fact, you might even have a better view than someone you think of as 'better' or 'more successful' than you. Who comes to mind? Taylor Swift? Elon Musk? A leader you admire? Maybe even a scientist planning a mission to the stars. Imagine, for a moment, that you have more power than they do because your view of the Moon is clearer.

I want you to feel what I felt as a kid. If you are following along, your perspective likely shifted when you ran this scenario through your head. You went from being alone in awe of the Moon to realizing you might have a better view, more access, and more power than you thought. With a simple shift in perspective, you moved from feeling limited to limitless.

My Moon-gazing practice marked the beginning of my discovery of life's most powerful lesson: we are born with the ability to see the world from different perspectives. We can shift our view and transform a situation that once seemed negative into something positive in an instant.

We are the creators of our reality, and our mindset is something no one can take from us. Others cannot control it or claim it; it's uniquely ours. When we nurture our curiosity and our minds—actively learning and expanding our thinking—there is nothing more powerful.

The ideas we choose to embrace shape our perspectives and behaviors, which ultimately determine the results we achieve. Yet, this is also why we often create imaginary boundaries for ourselves—self-imposed barriers that we feel holding us back, but that don't truly exist.

If you stay open-minded and curious, always asking questions, you'll find that life is constantly teaching us—though we can sometimes refuse to continue learning. With an open mind, every person, situation, and moment becomes a chance to grow. Every roadblock can turn into a bridge. External barriers are only manifestations of our own internal limitations.

This brings us to a powerful principle: there is no ceiling to what we can achieve, individually or collectively. Yet, we often lose sight of this truth. Achieving remarkable things requires constant reminders of our limitless potential and the ability to transform limitations into opportunities. Let's explore how to do exactly that. My mission here is to show you that any limitations you perceive are merely illusions.

Why anything is achievable

When I suggest that anything is achievable, you might well be skeptical, but I know it is true because I have proof. When you think about it, so do you. Just think about the world we live in. Many things once thought impossible now exist.

Today, we can fly through the sky—a feat once unimaginable. When aboard an airplane, I often look out the window, marveling at the clouds and the wonder of cruising through the air in these incredible machines. Before the last century, powered human flight seemed impossible, yet the Wright brothers, Orville and Wilbur, defied skeptics to achieve it. In 1903, they made history with the first powered, controlled flight in an aircraft, marking the beginning of a revolution in global transportation.

And then there's the internet. Once just a wild idea, it's now woven into daily life, powering almost everything we do. From checking our devices in the morning to working in front of screens all day, we're constantly connected. While that has both upsides and downsides, it does allow for us to access whatever information we need at any given moment on-demand, and we are always able to reach out to people that matter to us anywhere in the world. Most of us carry wireless-enabled devices in our pockets, some strapped to our wrists as smart watches, keeping us plugged into a world that would only recently have seemed a work of science fiction.

Throughout history, countless people have pushed boundaries and reshaped humanity through vision, belief, and action—despite the odds being stacked against them. From Marie Curie's groundbreaking scientific contributions (despite being a woman in a then-male-dominated domain) to Nelson Mandela's role in ending apartheid (after enduring 27 years of incarceration), the lesson of these peak human achievements is clear: you are capable of extraordinary feats if you are willing to challenge your perceived limits.

Science reveals a world filled with fascinating possibilities, inviting us to explore deeper and question what we know. For instance, we now understand that humans are made of atoms, which contain protons, neutrons, and electrons. Delving further, protons and neutrons are built from quarks, held together by forces carried by particles known as bosons—the fundamental carriers of nature's forces, which are energy waves. This realization underscores that everything around us, including ourselves, is made of elementary particles, energy waves, and the complex interactions between them. Such insights remind us of how much lies beneath the surface of what we perceive.

Our senses gather information, but it's our brain that organizes these signals to create our experience of reality. We see people, trees, the

Moon, and stars through this perceptual filter, constructing a unique view of the world. This filtered perception or worldview is our personal interface with reality, shaped by our sensory limitations and our brain's processing power.

This concept can be mind-boggling, yet it becomes clearer when we consider how non-human species experience the world differently. Take dogs, for example—they rely heavily on their powerful sense of smell, perceiving layers of scent that are undetectable to us. Our sensory limitations are significant; we only detect a fraction of the full range of information around us.

Science and technology have continually pushed these sensory limits, reshaping our perception and expanding what we consider achievable. The more we question and explore, the more we realize how much potential lies beyond our current understanding. This exploration, driven by curiosity and innovation, embodies the true essence of human achievement.

Einstein once stated that nothing can travel faster than the speed of light. However, with the discovery of quantum entanglement—where particles separated by vast distances affect each other instantly— scientists now recognize that certain types of information appear to move much faster than light.

There is always a limit to what is commonly considered possible and a boundary to push. The way the impossible becomes possible is—and has always been—through *us*. We have the power to challenge reality. All it takes is an unshackled mind, because the only things we can't do are the things we can't imagine. Once we imagine, that's the first step to turning an idea into reality. Everything humanity has created started as an idea.

I once thought, *If there's a limited amount of energy on Earth, why not mine the Moon for resources to create energy abundance?* Abundant energy would mean we wouldn't have to fight over it. This abundance mindset gave rise to Moon Express. When I moved on to my next project, I began questioning the structures of Western healthcare. Why are we focused on treating sickness instead of ensuring everyone enjoys a long and healthy life free from disease? This led to my current company, Viome, which contributes to a world of affordable, personalized, preventive healthcare.

It's easy to look at innovators or people who have launched successful initiatives and think, *They're not me*, but the only difference is that they remind themselves that *anything is possible*. Being open-minded and thinking differently is the first step to making the impossible possible. Science supports this with a simple principle of human behavior:

What you think → dictates what you do → which leads to what you get

Look at any action you take, and you'll see a relationship between what you think, what you do, and the results you get. For instance, consider your cup of morning coffee. You probably drink it because you wake up and think, *I need coffee before I can get started today*. You feel tired and crave that jolt of caffeine. And you get that jolt when you drink your morning brew. For many, this is so ingrained that they hardly notice the thought—they head straight to the coffee machine without hesitation.

Now, imagine you learn that coffee is harmful. Suddenly, your thoughts change: *Coffee is bad for me*. This new thought might make you feel wary, and as a result, you might skip it altogether. And now that you're not hooked on coffee you might even have *more* energy, and get more done. This example illustrates how our thoughts influence our actions and lead to the outcomes we produce. Change the thought, and you change the entire cycle.

It's also important to remember that every innovation started as a thought. The Wright brothers thought *it must be possible to make flying vehicles*, which led to their aeronautical actions. Even after many failures and self-doubt, they kept going, either because they believed it was possible or because, despite doubts, they continued to take action. This is the science of shaping reality—how we think and act shapes the results we achieve.

The bottom line is that it's to our advantage (and humanity's) to think counterintuitively. The more we question, stay open-minded, and push boundaries, the more we learn that limitations are simply gateways to the next world of possibility. Once you get curious about your thinking, you'll find there's an art to turning any issue into an asset and any roadblock into a new problem to solve. The questions you ask are the problems you solve. So, if you feel stuck, it may just mean it's time to ask a different question.

Turning barriers into opportunities

The first time I saw snow, I was wearing loafers with holes in them. I had just moved to the U.S. and was on my way home in Flemington, New Jersey. Out of nowhere, tiny white flecks started drifting from the sky.

For a moment, I just stood there, completely bewildered. *Do I need an umbrella?* My brain raced through all the possible explanations as I squinted at the sky, trying to read some secret message. I probably looked ridiculous standing there, staring up with my mouth half open as snow settled on my nose.

I had first landed in the States four months prior, in late summer. I felt like I was winning at life. I had made it to America! I'd found this charming old farmhouse to share with four friends and coworkers. It was surrounded by maple trees, lush green fields, and a sky that stretched endlessly, showcasing the most gorgeous sunsets. But now there were these tiny ice speckles falling on me. I had heard of snow, of course, but experiencing it for the first time was like an unexpected plot twist. I wasn't prepared for it.

As I walked home, snowflakes fell all over me, even finding their way into the holes in my loafers. By the time I arrived, my socks were soaked. The discomfort was compounded by the fact that the house had no insulation. When the four of us first moved in, we didn't know to check for insulation or ask about it; in India, it was never a concern. I don't even know if my father, a building inspector, would have thought to check. Where I am from, winter temperatures rarely fall below 60°F (15.5°C). Any New Jersey native would have immediately noticed the glaring oversight.

That first experience with snow led to many cold nights in that house. Time and again, I asked myself how I had ended up there. I became so miserable that I almost packed up and went back to India—which would have been a huge mistake.

Yet that chilly house taught me how to thrive in discomfort, to see obstacles not as roadblocks but as stepping stones. Your circumstances do not define your destiny—your mindset does. Adversity fuels creativity, and when you're down to nothing, you tap into everything that actually matters: your ingenuity, your grit, your hunger to dream big. Above all, it proved that you don't need ideal conditions to create extraordinary outcomes. You just need to believe it's possible—and then act like it.

I had many moments like this when I first came to the U.S. and during my early career. I hit roadblock after roadblock. But these experiences taught me that limitations can open the door to new worlds of possibility. Every roadblock teaches a lesson. We learn something new, and if we're smart, we can use our mind to see the same situation in a new way.

Over the years, I developed three methods to turn a perceived limit into a stepping stone:

1. **Turn shortcomings into assets:** At any moment, you can choose to see a challenge from an empowering perspective. By taking ownership of the issue and reframing it as an asset, you gain immediate control and can leverage the situation to your advantage.

2. **Reframe barriers as problems to solve:** Getting curious about what's holding you back and viewing it as a solvable problem can help you reclaim control. This mindset shift sparks fresh motivation and the energy to overcome the obstacle.

3. **Claim it to conquer it:** To truly overcome a barrier, first acknowledge and own it. This sense of ownership empowers you to confront and conquer the challenge directly.

There's an art to applying these methods effectively, so let's explore each one more closely.

Method 1: Turn shortcomings into assets

When I mentor entrepreneurs, a common problem I see is they have an insecurity holding them back, which is often actually an asset.

One common roadblock (where I have some expertise) is speaking English with an accent. Many people fear public speaking or being on camera because they think they have a 'weird' voice, lack expertise, or don't look 'right' (in their mind, unattractive). To this, I always ask them, "Have you heard *me* speak?"

My voice is unique, and it's clear I'm an Indian immigrant. There have been many times I could have felt self-conscious about how I sound or look. I could have chosen to stay quiet on issues that matter to me and the world. But instead, I embraced my voice and appearance, seeing them as the assets they truly are.

Because my voice is different, it stands out—it's iconic. My accent encourages people to slow down and listen closely, giving me their full attention. Being an immigrant also helped early in my career, making me memorable because I didn't sound or look like everyone else.

Embrace being different. It makes you unforgettable. People are often trying to fit in by looking and acting like everyone else. Yet, the people we remember are those who stand out. Plus, if you are spectacularly good-looking, famous, or wealthy, how do you know people want to know you for you?

Turning an issue into an asset starts by asking yourself what is good, useful, or advantageous about what seems to hold you back. This can be done with any perceived limitation. Often, these limitations turn into self-fulfilling prophecies: if you believe you have a problem, your actions will reinforce that belief.

For instance, if I had chosen to believe my voice was weird and avoided speaking on video, from stages, or to my company, there would be no InfoSpace, Intelius, Moon Express, Viome, or the philanthropic projects that have impacted billions. There would be no *Counterintuitive* book! Or, if I had only written books out of fear of public speaking, who would read them without my voice and visibility?

Embracing what makes us different helps us identify powerful opportunities to make a lasting impact.

The problems you perceive as holding you back will indeed hold you back—it's a scientific fact. When you believe something is a limitation, your actions will often reinforce it as your truth. But if you're willing to pause and think, *Why do I feel held back?* and consider how this reason might be an asset, what possibilities could you discover?

Now, think of an issue that is stopping you. Too old? Too young? Lack knowledge? Identify it, and let's turn these issues into assets.

- **Too old?** You have more wisdom, a broader network, and likely greater financial resources. You also have a greater sense of urgency, purpose, and conviction. Case studies and statistics often show that older CEOs are more likely to succeed.

- **Too young?** Being young allows you to ask for help and puts you in positions where you're expected to learn and grow. If you're building a business, consider young people who have defied the odds, like Mark Zuckerberg and Justin Bieber. You're well-positioned to build relationships with mentors who don't see you as competition. You have time! You can fail, get back up, and keep going. Plus, you're likely more tech-savvy than older generations.

- **Lack knowledge?** What I mean by this is being a non-expert on a topic. Without the presuppositions that come with expertise, you can see what others don't. You can use your lack of knowledge to innovate! In most of the businesses I've built, I wasn't an industry expert (we'll dive deeper into this in Chapter 9). Also, when you accept what you don't know, you can seek out those who do and learn from the best.

It is up to you to make your problem an asset. Generally, this requires a choice. You must choose to reject limitations and ask, "How can this issue actually work in my favor?"

Even if you don't see something as an asset, it can still be valuable if others do. Their beliefs about you can shape your reality, as their thoughts and actions influence the opportunities that come your way. People often spend enormous time and money trying to change aspects of themselves that, with a different perspective, might be seen as strengths rather than weaknesses.

Method 2: Reframe barriers as problems to solve

When I came to the U.S., people assumed I was a programmer, because many people from India were at the time. But I had never seen a computer in my life. However, I accepted programming jobs because that was what was offered to me, and I was limited. I quickly realized that I was not good at programming. I also had no desire to be a programmer. My skills were in sales.

So, one day, I went to the owners of the company where I worked and told them I'd like a role in sales. They said: "Naveen, how will you be good at sales if you can't speak proper English?" I was told it wasn't going to happen.

This was a moment where I could have easily stopped, but I got curious. I asked myself: *How can I stay in the country I love, keep my job, and use more of the skills I enjoy and am good at?* I focused on the outcomes I wanted to achieve and the barriers in the way. Then I used creative thinking to turn the barriers into a problem to be solved.

I pitched the owners another idea. I invented a better position that was useful to the company. I told them I could be a 'sales technician,' which meant I would help salespeople sell by helping them understand technical aspects of a product. A salesperson would do the talking, but I got the job done, and this allowed me to pivot from programmer to sales support.

Eventually, I became so good at this job that I realized I didn't need the sales guy. He was only there to make himself look good while I did all the work. I realized I could start my own company, which led to my first successful business—another barrier that I reframed as a problem that needed solving!

My first idea for a company was to build an internet business, because the web was new and exciting and more people needed to capitalize on the opportunity. This was in the early days of Web 1.0, where nascent web browsers had limited features. A big problem at the time was finding people's phone numbers. There was no easy way to do it. You had to call a specific number for directory assistance, and a human operator would ask questions to help you find the number you needed. However, directories weren't always helpful because people did not know or have the information they needed, such as the full name of the person they wanted to reach or the city in which they were located. It was a problem I saw needed solving, and I wondered if I could build a digital solution. It would be a platform where you can type any name or place, and it would give you the person's phone number, like the White Pages. I knew there would be a massive market. That was my first idea. I ran with it and it was my first major success.

I began to realize that the best business ideas often first appear as roadblocks or issues that irritate you and those around you. By getting curious about these problems, you can become the person who creates the product or service that provides a solution for many. This mindset is how I discovered my second massively successful business idea, which grew into a multi-billion-dollar company.

One day, while on a flight, I struck up a conversation with the woman sitting next to me. As we chatted, I asked about her job, and she mentioned she worked at AT&T. Intrigued, I asked more questions.

After a moment's hesitation, she explained that she was part of a team developing phones capable of connecting to the internet. At the time, this was a groundbreaking concept—enabling users to access the internet directly from their phones.

I started to think about how people might use this new feature. One of the first ideas that came to mind was searching for phone numbers, and I suggested they could pre-load the phones with a directory of numbers. She seemed to like the idea and promised to share it with her boss.

A few weeks later, I received a call from her. Her boss was impressed by the concept but had one concern: What if customers thought the company was giving out their personal information? To address this, he proposed a solution. If I agreed, they would include our company name on the packaging and the phone itself, making it clear that the feature was provided by our company, not AT&T. I accepted, and that decision marked the start of something groundbreaking.

What began as a simple suggestion to solve a problem led to the development of internet content on phones—a technology that hadn't existed before. That initiative grew rapidly, and we soon created the largest content provider for cell phones, building a company that eventually reached a value of $40 billion.

People think you have to be brilliant to make a billion-dollar company, but that's not the case. I achieved success because I learned to see roadblocks as problems to be solved. Over the years, these lessons evolved into a practice of being curious. Anytime you notice a roadblock for you and others, turn it into a problem to solve by asking *what would it take to eliminate this as a problem?*

The third way to turn problems into opportunities is through taking ownership of an idea.

Method 3: Claim it to conquer it

I think of all people as fitting into one of three categories. These are:

1. **Problem spotters:** These are people who can identify problems. In fact, all human beings are natural problem spotters because we naturally recognize issues.

2. **Innovators:** These are people who are very good at identifying solutions to a problem. They include strategic thinkers like visionaries, coaches, and consultants.

3. **Entrepreneurs:** These are the people who go out and do something about a problem. They don't just identify a solution; they actually *create* one.

To some extent, we all spend time in each category at different times in life. However, more people could take on the role of being an entrepreneur. While recognizing a problem is an essential first step, and thinking of solutions is important, nothing changes if no action is taken. Often, when people see a problem, they ask, "Why can't someone *do something* about this?"

Being an entrepreneur means being willing to take ownership of a situation or problem. It's how you shift from feeling like a victim to becoming powerful in an instant. It means asking, "What can *I* do to solve this problem?"

Now that we've discussed turning limits into problems to be solved, how do you ensure these barriers don't hold you back? The ultimate way to access the superhuman confidence, resilience, clarity, and power within us all is to have a *purpose*.

Purpose—not passion—is your rocket fuel

Enthusiasm isn't something you can manufacture. It's a genuine emotion that comes from meaningful ideas. If you pursue goals that don't resonate deeply or feel worth risking everything for, you won't wake up feeling enthusiastic about life.

Many people devote their time to missions that don't truly matter to them. They sell products they don't believe in and focus on questions like, "How can I build this business as quickly as possible to make money?" or, "What shortcuts can I take to get people to buy from me?" This kind of quick-fix thinking will never lead to deep fulfillment or long-lasting success. You might create a business that is profitable, but it won't be truly rewarding.

A lot of people talk about passion. But passion is nowhere near enough; *obsession* is what you want. Passion is for hobbies. Real entrepreneurs have an obsession, and not with things or people. They have an obsession with solving problems. Passion is a weak force because every time you encounter an obstacle, you can back off, and find a new passion. But, when you are truly obsessed with solving a problem, you go to bed thinking about it and wake up thinking about it.

We've already thought about what you're able to jump out of bed for, but let's go a step further: what cause would you be willing to die for? This might sound extreme, but it helps you cut through distractions and focus on what truly matters. Find out what that is, claim it, and pursue it unapologetically.

The ability to answer this question will become one of your most valuable assets. Too many people live without a meaningful mission, which means living without context or intention. Without this focus, it's easy to feel stressed, get sidetracked, and struggle with priorities.

Resistance fades quickly when you have a big purpose to pursue. Once you set your eyes on a goal that is meaningful to you—and this is key—every obstacle becomes a tiny speed bump. The best part of having a compelling purpose is that it draws people together to help make your dream a reality. You'll be amazed at how top talent aligns with a big shared vision. People will leave their jobs to join you, and resources will flow toward making your dream happen.

Beyond my opinion on this, there are a number of scientifically backed reasons why we should all get serious about living purposefully. Here are six:

1. **Amplified motivation:** Purpose unlocks drive and motivation, making you unstoppable in creating and building.

2. **Superior health:** When you're deeply passionate, you're more likely to take care of your health. Do you want a reason to stay healthy? Have a purpose. In my exploration of this topic, I have also found that those who don't have a purpose deal with more health issues.

3. **Increase longevity:** Purpose consistently appears in longevity studies and is recognized across cultures under different names because it universally matters. With a purpose, you will likely live longer.

4. **Deeper relationships:** Having a purpose drives us to seek out others, helping us build meaningful connections. Often, the best relationships come from a shared purpose.

5. **Mental resilience:** When you have a purpose, you are more eager to tackle roadblocks that get in your way.

6. **Wealth:** You are more likely to succeed in business if you have a greater purpose other than making money. Money is a byproduct of improving lives. If you want to make millions focus on a problem that helps a million people. The same is true if you want to reach the billion-dollar mark in business.

Many evolutionary biologists suggest that a sense of purpose drives humanity toward collective advancement—fueling innovation, cooperation, and long-term societal gains.[1] And research consistently

---

1   Frankl, Viktor E. *Man's Search for Meaning.* Boston: Beacon Press, 2006; Steger, Michael F. 2009. 'Meaning in Life' in *Oxford Handbook of Positive Psychology*, edited by Shane J. Lopez and C.R. Snyder, 679–87. Oxford: Oxford University Press.

shows that people lacking a sense of purpose face increased rates of depression, anxiety, disconnection, and even physical decline.[2]

You've likely already felt the power of purpose. Think back to a time when you were the most powerful version of yourself. At that moment, what was your purpose? I guarantee you had a deep desire to achieve an important outcome. For example, for any parent, the moment they have a child, there is an unyielding drive to work for the offspring's survival and future. As you read this, pause and think of a moment like that from your life. What did it feel like? You'll understand what I mean.

Of course, many people struggle with finding their purpose. I see this often with the entrepreneurs I mentor. They frequently face challenges in their business because they aren't truly invested in solving the problem—they're focused on the money they make from solving it. And why did they choose to pursue it? The answer is often survival.

Most people prioritize money over purpose because they need it to live. The key is to combine the two. Start with purpose. Choose a goal that is meaningful to you, first and foremost. Be intentional with your time. Second, ensure your goal is tangible and achievable—we'll discuss that soon in Chapter 5.

There is no sky

My father didn't always appreciate my entrepreneurial spirit. It wasn't until much later in life, after I'd proven myself, that he began to see me differently. My mom, though, always had an unbelievable amount of faith in me. When my dad would say, "You're not going anywhere,

---

2   Hill, Patrick L., Nicholas A. Turiano, Daniel K. Mroczek, and Brent W. Roberts. 2016. 'Purpose in Life as a Predictor of Mortality Across Adulthood' in *Psychological Science* 22(3): 391–98; Kim, Eric S., Carol D. Ryff, Jennifer K. Loving, and Jackie Smith. 2014. 'Purpose in Life and Reduced Risk of Alzheimer's Disease' in *Archives of General Psychiatry* 71(5).

so why try? Just get a degree in accounting," my mom would shake her head and reply, "No, no, no! Our boy is very smart. He can do anything he wants. The sky's the limit."

As I later learned, the sky isn't actually a physical barrier—that's a product of our imagination—simply a concept we've created! In her own unique way, my mom was telling me that imagination is the only thing that truly limits us. Our dreams, our vision, and how big we allow ourselves to think are the only real barriers. In a sense, we each create our own sky.

We can make and then break these imaginary boundaries for ourselves. We reach a goal and look back, realizing that what once seemed insurmountable was all in our minds. The barriers didn't actually exist—they were ideas that we bought into, shaping the limits we imposed on ourselves.

One of the most precious resources on planet Earth is the intellectually curious human being. Once you tap into your intellectually curious nature, there is nothing that you can't achieve. And if we all do this together, there is nothing we can't make happen. We only need to harness the curiosity to look at the world not as *is* but as it *could be*.

So, whenever you feel like you've reached your limits, remember that there is no problem that can't be solved by asking the right questions. There is no real limit to what you can achieve—no 'sky.' The barrier and the way forward are both within you. It's simply a matter of perspective.

Conventional thought trap

Most people believe they are limited, but the true barrier is created by accepting our self-imposed limitations. In reality, there are no limits, as countless boundary pushers have proven by reshaping the world.

Counterintuitive approach

Your limitations are not obstacles but gateways to identifying problems that need solving. They offer insight into what's possible and can be your most valuable assets when leveraged to your advantage.

CHAPTER 5

COUNTERINTUITIVE BUSINESS

"Whenever I run into a problem I can't solve, I always make it bigger. I can never solve it by trying to make it smaller, but if I make it big enough, I can begin to see the outlines of a solution."

—U.S. President Dwight D. Eisenhower

IN 2015, MY company, Moon Express, made history as the first private enterprise to receive U.S. government approval to leave Earth's orbit and land on the moon. This groundbreaking achievement went beyond the accomplishments of spacefaring nations like the U.S., Russia, and China. More than just a technical success, Moon Express was a bold statement: it proved that a small, ambitious team could achieve what was once the domain of nations. This milestone signaled a shift, showing that entrepreneurs—not governments—are now at the forefront of leading humanity into the future.

Yet beyond the magic of the mission itself, Moon Express offered me a profound personal insight: Big goals are easier to achieve than small ones.

This was an idea I had encountered before, but Moon Express showed me just how true it was. By expanding my thinking, I found that ambitious goals generate their own momentum. As we pursued the bold vision of landing on the Moon, doors opened, the right people arrived to help, and competition was minimal—because others simply weren't thinking as big.

It was a powerful reminder that an audacious goal is often more effective than a modest one. Scale up your thinking by an order of magnitude, or even by several orders as we did at Moon Express, and the world starts to meet you there, providing exactly what you need along the way. People don't just get excited; they're inspired. They want to be part of something larger than themselves, and if that's your project, expect them to knock on your door and find you.

People thought I was crazy for taking on Moon Express, often asking, "Why would you even *want* to go to the Moon?" Many assumed it was impractical or just a flashy PR stunt. But when I shared our true purpose, their perspective shifted. In fact, there were three very practical and compelling reasons.

First, as John F. Kennedy once said in his speech at Rice University:

> We choose to go to the Moon in this decade and do the other
> things, not because they are easy, but because they are hard,
> because that goal will serve to organize and measure the best
> of our energies and skills, because that challenge is one that we
> are willing to accept, one we are unwilling to postpone, and
> one which we intend to win…

I shared that sentiment in so many ways. Yes, it was hard, but it was also worth doing because it held great promise. The Moon contains vast reserves of valuable minerals. At Moon Express, one of our main goals was to land a rover on the Moon to mine helium-3, a rare element with the potential to meet Earth's energy needs for centuries. Our aim was to contribute to abundant, sustainable energy for everyone.

Second, while many were focused on preserving Earth, I was focused on preserving humanity. Think of it this way: eight billion of us (and counting) are living on this single fragile celestial body, vulnerable to any number of catastrophic events—whether a large asteroid, environmental collapse, or even our own actions. But the Moon is a neighbor that could become Earth's 'eighth continent.' By learning to live on the Moon, we could tackle many of the challenges we'd also face on planets like Mars, paving the way for human life to reach and potentially colonize places like Europa, Titan, or even planets beyond our galaxy. When we consider space and its potential to form part of our living environment, we unlock access to vast new lands and resources, reducing conflicts driven by scarcity.

Lastly, our vision was to make space travel affordable. Imagine buying a round-trip flight to the Moon—perhaps for a weekend getaway or a literal honeymoon. Why can't we be a multi-planetary society? When you think of all the 'impossible' things we now take for granted—cars, the internet, cell phones—you realize that what seems impractical today will form tomorrow's reality.

Before Moon Express, many assumed that humanity was confined to Earth, which led to a mindset of scarcity. But by thinking differently, I realized that scarcity is often a mental construct, not an actual limitation. Limits arise when we believe something isn't possible. But when we set big, ambitious goals, we inspire ourselves and others to look for solutions instead of accepting constraints.

Thinking too small is a pitfall I see far too often. Even in entrepreneurial circles, I hear mentors giving advice like "Just start," "Take the first step," or "Launch the website." While taking the first step is helpful to get moving, it's small thinking that causes many people to stop at the first obstacle. When people lack a bold, inspiring vision, they lose motivation and give up more easily when they face setbacks.

The vision and purpose we choose to pursue should be bold and exciting. It should deeply matter to us. That sense of meaning and urgency becomes easier to generate when our goals are big enough to stretch us. We need to aim at solving the impossible. When we do, we discover that it is indeed easier to achieve something audacious, something that can impact billions of lives.

If people don't think your goal sounds crazy, then you're simply not thinking big enough.

The magic of an ambitious mission

Picture this: My friend Daniel and I are at a party, and we're introducing ourselves in a circle of new acquaintances.

Daniel goes first: "Hi, I'm Daniel and I run a company that's building an iPhone app to help people find roommates."

Then it's my turn, and I say: "Hi, I'm Naveen. I'm focused on eliminating all chronic illness from the face of the Earth using food as a medicine."

What is more inspiring? An app for finding a roommate or a venture that creates solutions that put an end to chronic disease? If you're like most people, you chose the second answer. You probably think my friend's work is worthy and useful and would likely wish him good luck on his journey. However, it is unlikely that you would get overly inspired or excited by his elevator pitch (unless you are desperate to find a new roommate).

This is what happens when you have a big audacious goal versus a small one. When pursuing a bold mission, there's magic to it. People get inspired. They want to be part of your mission. When you share a giant vision, people start to rally around it in a way they never would for an ordinary or mundane goal.

People often wonder how it is possible to solve big problems like going to the Moon or treating chronic diseases. They think that's *much harder than anything I could do!* But these things are easier than they realize. After launching multiple companies in vastly different industries, I've learned there are seven reasons why big goals beat out small ones every time.

1. Personal investment

Big goals are generally more meaningful because they connect to our deepest desires as humans. It's at the core of human nature to want to do work that matters in the world and contribute to the lives of others in positive, profound ways. Big goals also fulfill the more egocentric reasons that drive people, such as financial abundance, recognition, and respect.

You may have also noticed that when you're emotionally pulled by a goal and have a deep desire to achieve it, life becomes much more fun. You feel energized. You want to jump out of bed in the morning and there is a biological basis for this. Beyond the surface, there are mood- and energy-boosting physiological chemical processes taking place. Audacious missions are more inspiring than small ones, and inspiration is a miraculous state.

In a state of inspiration, multiple brain systems are activated, leading to a cascade of positive emotions, creative thoughts, and a desire to leap into action. You get better at imagining future possibilities. Creative thinking is ignited. When you're inspired, your body produces more serotonin and dopamine, which are neurochemicals that are part of the brain's reward system.

These chemicals make you relentlessly pursue what you want.

Then, when you produce positive results, you get even more inspired. And even if the results aren't exactly what you want, you are still more likely to keep taking action because you are inspired. That is because inspiration boosts motivation. It activates a part of the brain responsible for goal-directed behavior and habit formation.

You will find that when you're inspired you are also more likely to connect with others and share your mission. And, then, they get inspired and want to take action too. By simply listening to you, they are likely to experience a similar brain chemical process when their mirror neurons fire, which can happen when people share ideas. You will find you become a magnet for the right people. These are the people you need to make your vision come to life.

2. Expert magnetism

When you have an inspiring vision, the best minds are drawn to your mission—from the experts who can make it happen to the investors eager to fund it. Intelligent people are motivated by challenging problems, and successful people seek significance. By tackling big challenges with you, they're creating something they can proudly call their legacy.

I've experienced this many times, and a perfect example is what happened when I launched my most recent company, Viome. In 2016, during a CNBC appearance, I announced my vision to make illness and aging a choice. Initially, I was there to discuss Moon Express's achievements, but the interview ran long, giving me the opportunity to share my next big idea. Seizing the moment, I made a bold, nationally televised declaration, even though I didn't yet have a fully detailed strategy. However, I did have a solid premise: with the science and technology available today, it should be possible to reverse disease states in the body.

A few days after my CNBC segment aired, I got a call from Guru Banavar, the head of IBM Watson Research. He had been working on the AI system I needed. He was compelled to join me because he had experienced firsthand what it was like to deal with a chronic incurable illness and have no solution. He had a daughter who had suffered from a cluster of symptoms ranging from fatigue, allergies, and various auto-immune symptoms during her high school years. She was given an idiopathic diagnosis, which means no one expert fully understood what was wrong. As a result, Guru became committed to building new solutions to treat chronic illness, from his lens of expertise, which is AI. He became our chief technology officer.

Another call I received was from Dr. Helen Messier, a microbiologist with a PhD and an MD in functional medicine, a healthcare approach that prioritizes uncovering the root causes of diseases. She was working with longevity trailblazer Craig Venter at the time, focusing on extending human lifespans. But she had a pivotal realization:

What's the point of living longer if those extra years are plagued by illness? Driven by this insight, she decided to leave her position and join us as our chief medical officer, in the mission to eliminate disease and help people achieve optimal health.

A few months later, I found my head of product strategy, Helene Vollbracht. While working as a marketing specialist for Uber, Helene heard me discussing Viome's mission on a podcast, and immediately felt drawn to it, recognizing how closely it aligned with her own passion for health. Helene was following the keto diet, which was wreaking havoc on her body. She'd already tried a range of trendy diets, from fasting to high-protein regimens, all in the pursuit of maintaining an ideal look. Without a deeper understanding of biology, Helene found herself in a cycle of restrictive eating, convinced that the less she consumed, the better she'd look. Like so many others, she was searching for answers outside herself, unaware that true change needed to start within.

I have many more stories of key team members and partners who, inspired by Viome's mission, reached out to join us. One of the most remarkable aspects of a mission-driven team like this is that each expert brings unique perspectives and a diverse set of skills to the problem.

Beyond that, building a team of individuals who are as driven as you are is crucial in making headway on a bold mission. It generates a collective resilience that helps you to remain steadfast in the face of challenges and build innovative solutions that make an impact.

3. Less competition

People who think bigger gain the advantage of being able to view problems from new angles and are more likely to create their own lane in an industry.

There are numerous examples of companies that have done this. Stripe simplified the financial complexity of online payments for businesses and became the go-to platform for digital transactions and e-commerce solutions. Airbnb disrupted the hospitality industry with a platform sharing peer-to-peer home accommodations, creating an entirely new experience in travel. These companies got out front and, even today, few competitors have been able to come close to their success.

Viome has also done this. When we launched, we had a bold mission to end chronic disease and to give people ways to avoid sickness and aging. This was very different from other healthcare companies, most of which have been designed to treat us when we are sick. We created a new lane and have become a leader in precision medicine and health products.

We are the only company offering at-home microbiome testing that delivers comprehensive physiological insights from stool, saliva, and blood—analyzed using metatranscriptomics and AI to reveal what your microbes are actually *doing*, not just which ones are present.

This data powered the creation of truly personalized supplements, giving your body exactly what it needs while eliminating guesswork. We are also leaders in oral microbiome health, with personalized toothpaste and lozenges designed to balance mouth pH—because many chronic diseases begin in the mouth.

Imagine you too are doing something that has never even been conceived of before, and certainly has never been attempted. You have data that challenges whole paradigms in your industry. You can see how quickly you can become someone who gets calls from reporters, influencers, and podcasters. Everyone wants to know what you're doing.

4. Media attention

Which of the following headlines grabs your attention and sparks your curiosity: 'How Three Roommates Built a Successful Short-

Term Rental Company' or 'How Airbnb's Founders Turned Rejection Into a $100 Billion Business'?

The second headline is clearly more compelling. It promises a powerful story of resilience, success, and triumph against the odds—all elements that draw people in. The first headline is flat and uninspiring. It doesn't have a unique angle. It doesn't give you a major reason to want to click or read more.

Media outlets exist to capture attention, and they know that stories of bold, unique pursuits sell. People chasing massive, impactful goals are natural headline-makers. Their stories are the ones we want to read because they tap into deep emotions like hope, curiosity, and admiration. Outlets prioritize these kinds of stories because they resonate with audiences, and bold, counterintuitive ideas have the power to cut through the noise.

When you're tackling a big challenge or breaking norms, reporters don't need to work very hard to find an angle—because *you* are the story. You naturally attract the media because people want to know what you're doing that's inspiring and out of the ordinary. And then, when the news spreads, you attract more of the people you need to make your cause happen. You widen your network.

5. Social capital

If you want to meet interesting people, *be interesting*. Social capital is critical, because when you engage with inspiring people, they'll connect you to fascinating opportunities, business collaborations, and even deep invaluable friendships that make your life better.

The minute you start to think, *everything is possible and I can achieve any dream I set out to accomplish*, amazing things happen. If you have people who are negative around you, you might see that you need to start spending time with more people who think optimistically. Cull people who laugh at your ambition and say you can't achieve it from your circle. Quite often, all you need to do is keep taking action and getting results and these people will disappear without you needing to do anything. You will find the people around you change naturally. You will align yourself with people who think at the same level.

It is important to remember that you become the average of the people you surround yourself with. Once you take big actions, people will react. The ones who believe in you and also think big will help you. Those who don't, won't. This will reinforce the identity shift that happens almost immediately when you declare you are taking on a massive mission.

6. Identity shift

Small goals and small actions are often harder to sustain because they're based on who we are today, not on who we want to become. When we set big goals, we naturally start to see ourselves in a new light—a shift in identity happens instantly. Suddenly, we're relating to life from the perspective of who we will be, not who we are right now.

Identity shift is a powerful way to create lasting change because it goes beyond surface-level actions and targets the core of how we see ourselves. When we shift our identity—our beliefs about who we are—our choices and habits begin to align with that new self-image.

Take this example: You turn 57 and catch a glimpse in the mirror that makes you realize you don't look as young or fit as you'd like. Like most people, you might think, *I need to get healthier.* Maybe you love chips too much, so the next day you cut them out, start going to the gym, and kick off a new regime. This routine might work for a few weeks or months, but often we fall back into old habits, struggling to make the change last.

Now imagine you take a different approach. You set a bold vision to be one of those 'fit 60-year-olds' who look decades younger. You tell your wife and friends, and you begin to see yourself as a 'SuperAger' or an 'Old Man Hottie.' By shifting your identity, you're far more likely to stick with these changes because you're relating to yourself differently—as a future version of you, vibrant and fit. This identity shift naturally inspires actions and behaviors that align with that vision.

The same process happens when you take on a bold, audacious mission. As soon as you declare it and share it with others, you become accountable not only to them but also to yourself. This shift creates momentum, inspiring greater and more impactful actions as you see yourself from a powerful place, already working toward your future self. Taking on a big goal puts you into a state of expanded possibility, helping you achieve remarkable results, whether you ultimately succeed or fail.

7. Expanded results

Setting extraordinary goals always leads to greater outcomes. By pushing the boundaries of what we believe to be achievable, we're compelled to design bottom-up strategies that demand creativity and bold decision-making. Such ambitious goals align teams, unify focus, and encourage innovation by forcing us to move beyond the status quo.

If you have heard of the idea of 'Big Hairy Audacious Goals' (BHAGs), as coined by Jim Collins and Jerry Porras in *Built to Last*, this will make sense. BHAG has become commonplace in many business circles. A great example is Microsoft's vision of 'a computer on every desk and in every home.' This idea challenged the Microsoft team to think far beyond incremental gains. It encouraged them to experiment, learn, and adapt. Big goals tend to bring out the best work ethic in people. Rigorous objectives lead to major breakthroughs.

When you think in a massively scaled-up way, however your specific project works out, you still win. You learn more profoundly and reach further. And along the way, all the other goals, like meeting interesting people, attracting the media, and personal fulfillment, are achieved.

The seven secrets in combination

These seven secrets have reciprocal and relational benefits where one builds and reinforces another. For instance, you are in the news to increase your chance of attracting more experts to help with your cause. Your social sphere is likely to widen with your media reach. Media recognition is then likely to further cement your personal resolve to solve the problem along with your new identity.

After exploring the seven secrets, it becomes clear that setting bigger goals can be both more rewarding and easier to achieve than aiming for smaller ones. But if big, bold missions have such potential, why don't more people pursue them? The answer often lies in self-belief— or the lack of it. People get a brilliant idea, only to shut it down with thoughts like *I can't* or *people will think I'm crazy*. Bold aspirations spark a mix of excitement and fear, a reaction that can easily discourage people from moving forward.

This is where Franklin D. Roosevelt's wisdom holds true: "The only thing we have to fear is fear itself." In moments of self-doubt, remember the lesson from Chapter 2: limitations are a doorway to boundless possibilities, and those limitations exist only in the mind. Take that first step, even if you doubt yourself—because, in many cases, you'll discover that you *can* succeed, and each small victory builds your confidence over time.

However, there is another way to avoid being paralyzed by fear: choose a massive purpose to pursue that is deeply meaningful to you. I emphasize this because it is critical. Your audacious goal must matter so much to you that you would die for it. When you commit yourself fully to solving a big problem *that matters to you*, you ignite an inspiration that drives you forward. Both inspiration and fear trigger the sympathetic nervous system, which is responsible for your 'fight-or-flight' response, but when you harness inspiration, it has the power to override fear. By focusing on what inspires you, fear dissolves.

Whatever this big idea is, it must hit a sweet spot where it has both *personal meaning* and *utility*. You can dream that a pig will fly, and this can really matter to you, but does it matter to others? If so, then you have a tangible reason to develop the idea. If your flying pigs can provide a low-cost, mobile workforce, for example, then your idea is justified by the savings it introduces at pork-powered Amazon Prime.

These types of bold missions are commonly referred to as 'moonshots.' However, the term has become overused and is thrown around without a deep understanding of what a moonshot is and how to craft one. Over the years, I have developed a three-question method for figuring out what bold audacious mission you can commit to that has both personal meaning and utility. It's called the 'Know Your Whys' framework.

How to craft a moonshot

If we're going to learn how to craft a moonshot, we should be clear on the definition.

A moonshot is an audacious goal that moves humanity forward. In business, I have heard other similar terms, such as 'Massive Transformational Purpose' (MTP) or the aforementioned 'Big Hairy Audacious Goal' (BHAG). However, I prefer the term moonshot because it signifies more than a massive goal or purpose. While it *is* both of those things, the key differentiator is that a moonshot defies conventional norms, moves humanity forward, and puts forth a vision and goal that (once realized) make the world better.

The term 'moonshot' originated with U.S. President John F. Kennedy's speech to Congress in 1961, in which he outlined the ambitious goal of landing a man on the Moon and returning him safely to Earth by the end of the decade. This vision, which culminated in the successful Apollo 11 mission in 1969, transformed the moonshot into a symbol of pursuing bold, seemingly impossible goals.

By my definition, a moonshot is a massive goal that must have the following four attributes:

- **It makes a new reality possible:** It is a goal that, once achieved, improves humanity by making a reality that once wasn't possible now possible.

- **It impacts millions of people:** A true moonshot solves a problem that impacts millions or even billions of people. This scale is critical to meeting the first criterion of creating a new reality.

- **It challenges conventional thinking and processes:** If you're not challenging norms you are not pushing the boundaries of what is possible.

- **The path to solving it is not straightforward:** You should not know how to solve a moonshot. If you are clear on how to solve a goal, it's a sign you're not thinking big enough.

Moonshots are more than big ideas; they are rallying calls to imagine and build a better world that many might think is impossible.

From my perspective, working on a moonshot is the only way to live. Why devote your time to anything less than an endeavor that truly matters—to yourself and to the world? I believe everyone is here for a purpose, not to lead a directionless existence. If you're not pursuing a meaningful goal, can you fully activate your potential, grow, and contribute? After all, that's what we're here to do.

Remember that a moonshot is not just about solving a major, meaningful problem. It is also how you achieve personal satisfaction in life. A moonshot drives you to leap out of bed in the morning. It energizes you, connects you with like-minded people, and ultimately leads to financial success because making money is a byproduct of creating value for others.

At this juncture, you might want to consider the current purpose(s) you're pursuing in life. Are you devoting your time and energy to solving problems that matter? Is your time being well spent?

If you're not completely sure of how to answer these questions, you probably don't have a clear vision for your moonshot, and that's the perfect place to be at this point in the book. Because next we'll explore my Know Your Whys framework for crafting moonshots.

The Know Your Whys framework

My Know Your Whys framework is a three-question process anyone can use to clarify a moonshot idea and determine if it's worth pursuing. The questions are:

- Why this?

- Why now?

- Why me?

These questions guide you through a strategic thinking process. *Why this?* allows you to focus on the idea's core purpose. *Why now?* brings clarity and urgency, helping you make the concept tangible. Finally, *Why me?* prompts you to explore your unique perspective and apply your counterintuitive thinking to the subject.

The ultimate outcome is confidence—the kind of conviction that solidifies your belief that the problem you're tackling is one you can solve. While others might think your idea is far-fetched, this framework equips you to explain the logic behind it. It also helps you stay committed when faced with doubt—a challenge that often stops brilliant visionaries from taking action.

Now, before you launch into the Know Your Whys process for crafting your moonshot, your first step is to make an exhaustive list of the areas and problems you see in the world. The massive goal you choose to pursue doesn't have to be in an area where you have expertise—this is important to understand as you begin creating your list.

Simply ask yourself, "What massive problems do I believe need solving?" How about world hunger? The environment? Chronic disease? Or, think about a massive issue within a larger area, like the mental health crisis in public health. Consider the divisiveness within or between nations. What about real education in schools? Issues of clean water or other resources? There are so many massive problems in this world to choose from, and even if we solve some, others will take their place.

For inspiration, consider searching online for 'world's biggest problems' or using an AI tool to generate ideas. Start by thinking broadly and listing everything that resonates with you.

Next, reflect on which areas or industries matter most to you. A helpful approach is to imagine waving a magic wand to transform the world. How would it look different? What specific changes would you prioritize?

As you ponder these issues, some will resonate more deeply than others. Certain problems may stir strong emotions or a sense of urgency within you. Pay attention to these feelings—they're a signal of an idea worth exploring. When a problem sparks that emotional charge, take the time to dig deeper. Use the Know Your Whys framework to assess whether this is a goal you'd be passionate about dedicating the next decade to pursuing.

Now, let's dive into the question: *Why this?*

Why this?

Select a problem you'd like to solve. Fast forward ten years into the future. The problem is now resolved. The area you chose to focus on has transformed. Imagine that the future you envisioned exists today.

When you ask *Why this?* from the perspective that you are actually successful in solving the problem that you set out to solve, would it help a billion people live a better life? It's not because you are philanthropic and just want to help a billion people; it's capitalistic. If you build a product or service that can help a billion people live a better life, you can create a $100 billion company. The reason is that the billion people whose lives are better because of your product or service become your loyal customers, allowing you to create a massive enterprise.

You shouldn't wake up thinking, *What should I do to create a $100bn company?* Instead think, *What can I do to help a billion people live better?* After all, making money is a byproduct of doing things that improve people's lives.

You should never focus on the world as it is. Focus on the world as it *could* be.

Two of my favorite prompts for this stage are 'what if' and 'imagine.' These simple words help dissolve preconceived limitations. For a moment, you can play in the expansive mind space of what *could* be possible. At this stage, the *how* isn't important. If you're focused on a truly transformative idea, you won't know exactly how to achieve it right away—and that's okay.

Don't let the tyranny of *how* stifle your vision.

It's a common trap. I've seen it happen time and again—people get excited when they identify an area that deeply resonates with them. They begin to formulate the vision, only to extinguish that spark by realizing they don't have all the answers.

Here's how this plays out: A moonshot thinker might have a thought like *education needs to change!* They picture their child trudging off to school, engaging with a rigid, outdated system that fails to inspire or ignite a love for learning.

They imagine that same child stepping into a rapidly changing world, where much of what they have been taught will hold little relevance. The need for a complete reboot of the public education system becomes clear to them.

But then, as often happens, that initial burst of inspiration is overshadowed by doubt. The excitement gives way to fear, as they think, *how could I possibly do anything to change this? Where would I start?*

This is where many people get stopped. But the key is not to let the absence of clear answers kill the dream. At this stage, figuring out how is not your job. Formulating a vision that speaks to you is. So, anytime you have a thought like that, do not give it power.

Suspend any notions of how and keep focusing on the vision of the new reality you want to see. Your job is to imagine, in very vivid detail, what the world would be like if your problem were solved. Use your imagination to visualize it in your mind or write it down if you would prefer.

It must be a vision you can articulate so vividly that others understand it immediately. Martin Luther King Jr. did this well.

In his famous I Have a Dream speech, delivered in Washington D.C. in 1963, he said:

> I have a dream that one day down in Alabama with its vicious racists, with its governor having his lips dripping with the words of interposition and nullification, one day right down in Alabama little black boys and black girls will be able to join hands with little white boys and white girls as sisters and brothers.

He asks us to envision a future of racial equality and unity, where children of all races can live and interact as equals, free from the prejudice and segregation of the past.

The moment you hear those words, you can picture the children walking together in your mind—it's instant and undeniable.

Your vision should have the same power to resonate and inspire.

John F. Kennedy was also a master at articulating moonshots. He once painted a vivid picture for the American people, declaring: "The United States is going to put a man on the Moon and return him safely to Earth within a decade."

With this statement, you could immediately imagine a space-suited astronaut traveling to the Moon in a rocket to plant the flag of the United States on its surface before returning safely home. At the time, no one—not even NASA—knew how to achieve this goal. President Kennedy didn't explain *how* it would be done; he simply knew it had to happen. He framed the vision with a clear purpose: the United States needed to surpass other nations in technology to protect itself and maintain its leadership on the global stage. The *why* was firmly established long before the *how*.

Let's go back to our education example. Let's imagine a world where every kid loves school because they are thirsty to learn. Imagine kids learning skills of the future, not skills that robots will replace. Most people, especially parents with school-age kids, will get the difference. It's a future they can buy into immediately.

When you think like this, not only do you create a vision you can connect to emotionally and believe in, you also share it in such a way that others *get it*. If you share your vision and people *don't* get it, you're not being clear enough.

Once you have your vision created for yourself in vivid detail, then ask: If you solve the problem you set out to solve, would it help a billion people live a better life? This question is about scalability. If you answer yes then you are focused on a problem that is worth your time and where you won't hit a ceiling in your growth. It will also be a problem that achieves the sweet spot of activating the seven secret benefits of taking on a larger-than-life goal.

At this stage, it's crucial to avoid defining your moonshot too narrowly or focusing on a specific solution. A moonshot should be a broad premise. For example, declaring, "I will build the first anti-gravity boots," might sound ambitious and groundbreaking. However, it is tied to a defined solution. Instead, ask yourself: *What are the limitations of personal travel and what would life look like if they could be solved?*

Your moonshot declaration could be reframed as: "I will revolutionize personal travel by making it easy, faster, affordable, and more fun." This broader premise avoids limitations, leaving room for pivots and adaptability. Focusing on the problem you want to solve, rather than a predefined solution, creates a more open and flexible foundation for innovation.

This is why our mission with Viome has always been to 'make illness and aging optional.' This premise enables us to prioritize preventative measures. Focusing solely on treating symptoms, as many other healthcare companies do, would limit our efforts to addressing illness only after it occurs, rather than helping individuals avoid it altogether.

Lastly, whatever future you see really needs to be worth it to you to pursue or it is not a great moonshot. Don't ask if the glass is half full or half empty. Instead, ask: Is this glass worth filling? Because if you believe it is then it doesn't matter if the glass is half empty or half full.

Solidify a vision you can commit to and believe in it. Again, you should not know how to solve it.

In fact, you are at an advantage if you're not a non-expert. Your ignorance is what makes you the best person to disrupt your chosen industry. When you're starting a new business, you don't need to know much about it. Most of the work is tactical and is common to most businesses. It is the same stuff no matter what sector you're in.

However, if you don't know much about the field, you're able to ask questions that an expert would never ask, and that allows you a very different thought process and a fresh approach. You can fundamentally challenge the foundation of what experts take for granted. This allows you to rethink and reinvent.

Besides, experts are generally terrible at predicting the future. Here is some evidence:

"There is not the slightest possibility of such journeys," American astronomer F.R. Moulston once said of humans going to the Moon.

"Heavier than air flying machines are impossible," Lord Kelvin, president of the Royal Society of London believed in 1895.

"There is no reason for any individuals to have a computer in their home," said Ken Olsen, founder of DEC computer company.

These bold (and completely wrong) predictions, as well as many similar examples, demonstrate that while experts excel at incrementally improving technology, disruptive ideas tend to come from non-experts. The more you know, the more barriers you see and the quicker you are to spot ways in which innovative ideas won't work.

There are not many examples of insiders disrupting an industry. This is a shame, because all it takes to transform any given industry is for someone with an open mind to ask, "Why can't we do it?"

Great examples include Uber's disruption of the taxi industry and Airbnb in the hotel industry. The same is true in healthcare. The pharmaceutical industry makes billions of dollars keeping you sick. As a rule, they don't sell cures, they sell symptom suppression and management. They want to ensure that you take their drug (and pay for it) for the rest of your life. But an entrepreneur who has no stake in the field sees a better way forward. This is why Viome has succeeded. At the outset I asked, "How can we prevent illness from happening in the first place instead of taking care of it after you get sick?"

When I launched Moon Express, I had absolutely no background in space exploration—I was a software guy. But that turned out to be an advantage. Because I wasn't burdened by traditional aerospace thinking, I brought the concept of modularity from software into the space sector. Historically, if you wanted to go to the Moon, experts would recommend building a single rocket capable of traveling to the lunar surface and returning. But from a software mindset, that approach seemed inefficient.

I saw the journey as three distinct modules. First, the Earth's gravity is intense, so you need a small and cheap rocket to get to low earth orbit. But once you're in low earth orbit, the environment changes— there's very little gravity so you can use a less powerful propulsion in the lander to take you to the moon orbit and use it to slowly land on the moon. Which means you don't need the same type of propulsion technology as the massive rocket, you could use something lighter. Finally, because the Moon's gravity is only one-sixth that of Earth's, a small, lightweight booster could handle the return from the lunar surface to Moon orbit.

It was only because I had no training as a rocket scientist that I asked: "Instead of one massive vehicle doing everything, why not use a small rocket to the low orbit and build a propulsion in the lander that takes off from the low earth orbit to land on the moon? The lander can carry the return vehicle with small propulsion to come back to Earth?"

That seemingly naive question challenged decades of conventional thinking. It disrupted the aerospace industry by introducing a modular approach to space transport—reducing costs and opening new doors for lunar exploration and commerce.

This experience taught me something invaluable: expertise is powerful, but it can also be limiting. Experts often carry the weight of how things have always been done. As an outsider, I was free to imagine how things could be. Sometimes, it takes not knowing the "rules" to rewrite them. If your ideas don't sound a little crazy to others, maybe you're not dreaming big enough. And when someone says something is impossible, remember—they're only revealing *their* limits, not yours.

How do you think big and believe in yourself while embracing being a non-expert or even being seen as a business lunatic? The key is grounding your vision in reality. Connect your bold idea to the world as it exists today. Conduct research to gather evidence and build a compelling case that your 'impossible' idea is not only possible but achievable within a realistic timeframe. This is the power of asking *Why now?*—the crucial second step in the Know Your Whys process.

Why now?

Why now? is the second piece of the moonshot puzzle. It's about assessing whether this is the right moment to tackle your problem in the way you envision.

This requires examining what has changed in the last few years and, more importantly, what you expect to change in the next three to five years that will allow you to solve the problem at scale. This should tell you why the problem couldn't have been solved five years ago. You don't want to be using yesterday's technology to solve tomorrow's problems, because by the time you are ready to scale, someone will solve it using the latest technology and disrupt *you*. You want to intercept the technological curve when it's growing exponentially, so you are ready to scale as technology is improving in price and performance.

If the tools to solve your problem already exist but the problem persists, it's likely because the solution isn't truly needed, or the necessary technology hasn't matured yet. Instead, focus on leveraging tomorrow's emerging technologies to address future challenges. Relying on yesterday's tools to solve tomorrow's problems is a fruitless endeavor.

Even with a solid idea and strong business model, success hinges on *when*, not just *how*, you enter the market. It may surprise you to learn that timing is the single most powerful predictor of a business's success. In one study, timing accounted for 42% of business outcomes across 150 companies and 45 IPOs and acquisitions.

Consider the success of Netflix, which began as a DVD rental mail service, just as people were growing frustrated with the late fees at brick-and-mortar rental stores like Blockbuster. Though the concept was innovative, Netflix didn't take off until it tapped into a deeper trend: people's desire for convenience and the early shift to online solutions. Timing was crucial; as broadband internet became more widely available, Netflix was primed to pivot from its mail-order model to streaming, aligning perfectly with the rise of digital content.

Another example is YouTube. The platform launched in 2005, just as consumer video technology was improving and social sharing was gaining momentum. Many dismissed the idea of people uploading personal videos for public viewing, but YouTube's timing was impeccable. With a user-friendly interface, and as one of the few video-sharing platforms available, YouTube thrived alongside increasing broadband speeds and the growth of social networks.

Even the best ideas can fail if launched at the wrong time. Successful ventures don't just address a demand; they align perfectly with a pivotal market moment, tapping into people's needs and behaviors at just the right time. So, is now the right time to bring your vision to life?

To answer this, start with research. When I explore an area that I want to positively disrupt, I immerse myself in learning. I dive into the industry's core, reading research papers and books, scouring the internet for insights, and talking to people with firsthand experience in the field.

If we use education as our template again, an exploration into the topic might lead to these types of conclusions:

- You notice from watching local and national news and reading national publications that the world seems to be talking a great deal about the public education system and how it needs to be reimagined.

- You learn that futurists believe that 60% of today's school kids will work a job as an adult that doesn't yet exist.

- You and everyone you know is using AI tools, so you are noticing certain skills will be redundant.

- As you delve deeper into this area, you see that government is the primary shaper of educational curricula. A new model operating outside the public system might require individuals to pay, which could present a significant barrier for widespread adoption.

- To advocate for change at the government level, you'll need to develop a comprehensive model and gather data to support your case for reforming the public system. Additionally, you'll need to assess the technologies learners will require, along with the resources, funding, and development necessary to implement these changes.

At this stage, you don't—and shouldn't—have all the solutions. However, you should understand the systems and resources you're working with, recognizing potential advantages, obstacles, or challenges that could make your vision difficult to realize. This awareness will encourage new ways of thinking, helping you identify initial steps to take, areas requiring further research, or key people to consult.

Asking *Why now?* is not just about establishing whether the time is right, it's also an opportunity to start thinking about your path ahead—particularly about making sure you can chart a way forward that is not blocked by critical barriers (ones you can't overcome, which we will tackle in the next chapter) that make your moonshot a futile pursuit because of insurmountable technological or societal limitations.

When I started Viome, I went through this process. It gave me confidence that this moonshot was a smart idea to pursue. I started with the premise of making illness and aging optional and dug into the research.

I was reading hundreds of health research papers and learned that microbiome and inflammation were related to chronic disease and aging. I started to think that if we can figure out what is causing inflammation and ways to reduce it, we can slow or eradicate disease states. We would need to be able to comb through and draw connections between large sets of biological data. I also saw that AI technology was becoming more affordable and mainstream, so we could use it to create affordable solutions.

I was also watching other technologies like genome sequencing drop in price, and this validated that the era of precision medicine was coming. In 2017, when Viome launched, it cost approximately $1,450 to get your genome sequenced. Seven years prior, it had cost $50,000, a price few people could afford. But as the cost dropped, it was soon within reach of most middle- to upper-middle-class consumers. The same trend would happen with AI. This was the perfect storm for innovation.

When you are thinking through *Why now?* consider major societal trends that are happening, technologies that are emerging, and dig into research in the industry of your moonshot. You will begin to see patterns that will help you decide if your idea is grounded in reality and if it is possible to make headway on it now. If you conclude the time is right, you can move on to the last step: *Why me?*

Why me?

What question are you asking that is different from what everyone else in the industry is asking? This is important to identify, because *the questions you ask are the problems you solve.* If you don't ask the right question, you will solve the wrong problem.

By asking slightly different questions, you find solutions that experts have yet to consider—because your problem was not the one they were trying to solve. Most innovations fail because they end up solving a symptom of the problem rather than its root cause. Sometimes solving the symptom may give you short-term success. But inevitably, someone comes and solves the root cause and then you're completely out of business.

When I was running Moon Express, I often told people that humanity will one day become a multi-planetary society. Inevitably, they'd ask me the same question: "How are you going to grow food on the Moon?" It's a valid question, but it's the wrong one. The problem with that question is that it assumes there's only one solution: finding a way to grow food.

By reframing the question slightly, we open up a world of possibilities. Instead of asking how we can grow food, we could ask: "Why do we need food?" The answer is that we need food for energy and nutrition. But if that's the goal, are there alternative ways to meet those needs? For example, plants derive energy from photosynthesis, while some bacteria thrive in environments like nuclear waste by harnessing energy from radiation.

When you shift the question, you get entirely new ways of thinking about the problem, unlocking diverse and potentially groundbreaking solutions.

So think about whether you are solving a symptom of the problem or its root cause.

Here's an example: The scarcity of fresh clean water is widely recognized as one of humanity's most pressing challenges. If you're an entrepreneur aiming to tackle this issue, you might develop a new nano-filtration system to turn dirty water into fresh water. While these solutions address the symptoms of fresh clean water scarcity, they don't address the root cause of the problem.

An entrepreneur focused on the root cause would ask a different question: "Why do we have a shortage of freshwater in the first place?" Upon reflection, you'd discover that the majority of freshwater is consumed by agriculture. Agriculture, therefore, is the underlying driver of water scarcity.

What if you developed hydroponic or aquaponic farming systems that use only a fraction of the water required by traditional agriculture? By addressing the agricultural demand for water, you're tackling the root cause of the problem and creating a more sustainable solution.

You can dive deeper into the root cause of water scarcity by asking yet again: "Why do we need so much agriculture?" and, "Where does the majority of agricultural production go?" Answering these questions reveals that much of the world's productive agricultural land is used to grow feed for cattle. This insight shifts the focus: solving the problem of water scarcity requires addressing the inefficiencies of raising cattle.

You might then ask, "Why not encourage more people to adopt vegetarian diets?" or, "How can we produce meat without raising cattle at all?" These questions open the door to innovative solutions. For instance, one approach is to use stem cells to grow muscle tissue directly in a lab, without the need for an entire animal. After all, people don't eat the bones, organs, or skin of cattle—we only consume the muscle tissue. By cultivating just the muscle tissue, you bypass the need for traditional cattle farming, dramatically reducing water use.

The exciting part is that these solutions aren't just theoretical—they're happening now. Innovative companies are using stem cells to create lab-grown meat, while others are developing plant-based proteins that mimic the taste and texture of meat. These advancements free up agricultural land and significantly reduce water consumption, offering a sustainable path forward for addressing water scarcity, especially in developing regions.

By reframing the problem and tackling the root causes, these ideas not only address water scarcity but also pave the way for more efficient and sustainable food systems. Just as importantly, producing meat from sources other than cattle may also benefit the environment, because cattle produce very harmful methane gas that causes global warming.

If you want to solve problems like these, it is helpful to adopt the curiosity of a two-year-old, always asking, "Why, why, why?" And then think about how you can approach the situation differently. Look at what other people are doing and ask different questions. Remember that the questions you ask are the problems you solve.

As you can see, the Know Your Whys framework requires a great deal of counterintuitive thinking. And if you see the power of it, but still think it's complicated for you to think this way, I have one last structure that naturally positions you to be a moonshot-sized thinker: Put yourself in environments where you are surrounded by people and places that expand you. I call these 'atmospheres of abundance.'

Atmospheres of abundance

There was a time, long ago, when I saw myself as a big fish in a small pond—that was when I lived in India. But everything changed when I moved to the United States. Here, I began meeting people from all walks of life, each with unique perspectives and talents. It wasn't long before I realized that I had stepped into a much bigger pond—and in it, I was just a small fish.

This shift in perspective led me to adopt a new practice: I made it a point to surround myself with people who I believed were better than me. I sought out environments that challenged me to think differently and pushed me to grow in the areas I wanted to improve. Over time, I discovered a simple but profound truth: the people you surround yourself with and the environments you spend the most time in are the most powerful forces shaping your thinking—and ultimately, your life.

Many people have heard the saying, 'You are the financial equivalent of your five closest friends.' While most people conceptually understand this, few take meaningful steps to evaluate their social circles or intentionally spend more time with people who inspire growth and success. This principle goes beyond finances—it profoundly impacts your mindset, habits, and overall quality of life.

Social influence doesn't stop at your immediate circle. The concept of 'three degrees of separation' in sociology demonstrates that we are influenced behaviorally and emotionally by people up to three connections away in our social network. This means your thoughts, feelings, and actions are shaped not only by your closest friends (one degree) but also by your friends' friends (two degrees) and even their friends' friends (three degrees). Beyond this third level, the influence typically diminishes, but within these boundaries, your network exerts a powerful effect on your behaviors, aspirations, and worldview.

Understanding the depth of social influence highlights how essential it is to choose your relationships wisely. Surrounding yourself with individuals who challenge you to grow, model positive behaviors, and embody the traits you admire—whether ambition, kindness, resilience, or creativity—can amplify your personal and professional development. These influences extend beyond your immediate relationships, creating a ripple effect that impacts your broader social network.

Conversely, staying in stagnant or negative environments reinforces habits and attitudes that can hold you back. By deliberately cultivating a network of people who uplift and inspire you, you not only transform your own life but also positively influence the lives of those connected to you within those three degrees of separation.

Your network doesn't just reflect who you are; it shapes who you become. To elevate your life, prioritize building relationships that encourage you to think bigger, aim higher, and expand your potential—not only for your own growth but for the ripple effect it creates within your community and beyond.

For example, starting a fitness routine might encourage friends who see and interact with you regularly to do the same. Your influence doesn't stop there, though. It extends to the friends of your friends: your dedication to fitness could inspire a friend's friend to get active, even if you don't know that person personally. Finally, there's a third, extended influence, which includes friends of friends of friends. Although weaker at this distance, your habit might still prompt someone you've never met to take up exercise.

Picture this: I'm hiking with my friend Richard Branson in the British Virgin Islands, something we love to do whenever we're both at our homes there. Richard had just wrapped up hosting an event on Necker Island with 40 entrepreneurs innovating in the wellness space. At the same time, I had been on a panel at a health summit in Scotland, exchanging ideas with some of the brightest minds in health.

As we hike, the conversations naturally flow, sparked by the inspiring people we've interacted with over the past week. Richard shares an insight that gets me thinking differently about a product line at Viome, and I share an idea that shifts his thinking about writing a longevity book—an idea he now feels driven to make a reality. Later, we both head home for dinner with our wives, where the energy from our conversation spills over. We share our excitement, which inspires new ideas for the projects our wives are passionate about. By the end of the evening, we're all more inspired, motivated, and connected than we were when the day began.

This is the power of three degrees in action. It's a perfect example of why spending time with people who expand you and immersing yourself in environments that encourage growth are so important.

Social phenomena like happiness, obesity, smoking, and even political views spread through social networks up to this three-degree limit. Your environment and those of people you engage with shape your thoughts, behaviors and actions. The impact of one individual can ripple out to affect society on a broader scale. And so, when you make an effort to put yourself in the right environment and with the right people, expansion happens naturally. It then becomes very easy to change and think bigger and differently. (We will discover more on this in Chapter 6.)

While connecting with peers is important, don't limit your growth by staying exclusively within your comfort zone. Take the initiative to connect with industry leaders and explore opportunities to engage with people in entirely different fields. Seek out mentors who can provide guidance, challenge your thinking, and inspire you to grow. Expose yourself to radically different environments and surround yourself with individuals who are achieving at a higher level than you. Being around such people will accelerate your growth, push you to think bigger, and teach you the methods and strategies they've used to succeed.

Also, reflect on the communities and places where you spend your time—whether it's where you live, work, or visit. The environments you immerse yourself in have a profound impact on your mindset and opportunities for expansion. Choose wisely and intentionally. Then, every day, ask yourself:

- Am I better intellectually today than I was yesterday?

- Am I emotionally better than yesterday?

- Am I spiritually better today than yesterday?

This structure is a very simple way to remind yourself of what you need to do to dramatically expand your thinking. Get used to asking yourself these things at least once a day, and they will soon become a very healthy habit.

Conventional thought trap

Most people limit themselves by thinking too small, which leads to uninspiring goals and average results. To unlock your true potential, you must think orders of magnitude bigger.

Counterintuitive approach

Big goals are easier and more satisfying to achieve because thinking bigger taps into purpose and momentum, attracts top talent, and allows you to carve your own lane where you create something truly remarkable for the world.

CHAPTER 6

COUNTERINTUITIVE LEADERSHIP (AND PARENTING)

*"It's not just about leaving a better world for our children,
but also, raising better children for our world."*

—Source unknown

IN 2024, I had more time than usual to pause and reflect on life. It was a milestone year for the Jain family, with two weddings and the addition of two new wonderful members to our family. I took a bit more time away from work than usual to deeply connect with family, old friends, and new people who are important to my children.

First, for my son Ankur's wedding, we embarked on an unforgettable journey to Africa where we watched elephants roam and cheetahs hunt. Then, we flew to Egypt where he was married at the foot of the ancient pyramids. Soon after, we came together again, but this time for my daughter Priyanka's wedding. Both Ankur and Priyanka also chose to honor tradition with additional ceremonies at our home in Seattle.

97

I found myself reflecting deeply on the lives my kids have built, what I'm most proud of them for, and my legacy as a father and leader. During the celebrations, I gave several speeches. At Ankur's wedding, I shared a sentiment that captures what my life is like as his dad. I shared a similar statement at Priyanka's wedding. And when Neil, my youngest, gets to his next big milestone, I will share how proud I am of him. Here is what I said: "What makes me proudest about Ankur is that wherever I go, people now know me as 'Ankur's dad'."

Each of my children has been incredibly successful at tackling major societal issues by approaching problems from a different angle and applying innovative solutions. For this, they've all been award earners and headline makers. The week of Ankur's wedding, we also celebrated seeing his face on the cover of *Forbes* magazines. A few weeks later, he was profiled in a spread in *People* magazine. As I was working on this book, we were cheering on his sister who was selected by the CEO of Goldman Sachs as a top female entrepreneur.

Ankur, a Wharton graduate and the founder of The Kairos Society, has transformed the lives of millions of renters who once felt they were spending their money away, never to be a homeowner, and struggling to build credit. His next company, Bilt Rewards, rewards renters for paying rent on time. It also helps them build credit towards the purchase of a home by offering a credit card that gives points for everyday purchases—like dining, travel, and more—that can be redeemed for rent, a future home down payment, or travel. Remarkably, he solved the issue of landlords rejecting credit card rent payments due to the 3% fee. He pitched MasterCard a bold idea to waive the fee specifically for rent, and they agreed! He made a model that works for both renters and landlords and has changed lives and given hope to millions.

Priyanka, a Stanford graduate and Mayfield fellow, is also on an ambitious mission to transform women's health. She's the CEO of Evvy, a pioneering company working to close the gender health gap by uncovering overlooked female biomarkers. Until 1993, women were excluded from clinical research, which has led to a widespread lack of understanding of female-specific conditions. It's an oversight that has made many drugs less effective and even harmful to women.

Neil is a Stanford graduate and a Schwartzman scholar. He is looking at the problem of housing from a different angle than his brother. He told his sibling: "Ankur, you keep focusing on rent, I'll focus on mortgages." So, he is now looking at reimagining how we finance our homes.

Now you get what I mean when I say I am proud to be known as my kids' dad. Each of them has built an impressive reputation for impacting humanity in profound ways, and each on their own terms.

My kids have already accomplished so much in their young lives, at a much younger age than their dad. I didn't build InfoSpace, my first successful company, until I was in my late 30s. My wife, Anu, and I, always said, "If our kids and the next generation are better than us, we can rest assured we have done our job."

Your success in this life will not be measured by what you do—it will be measured by what you do to make the next generation better. It is the job of every person to not only leave this world better for the next generation but to *make the next generation better for the world.*

The focus of this chapter might seem to be on parenting, but really this is about leadership through a counterintuitive lens. Parents are the leaders in their families and, in a strange way, leaders are the parents in their workplace. Many of the principles that apply to one are also relevant to the other.

So, consider the roles you play in the world from a new, expanded, perspective. You will see that the lessons here for parents equally apply to you as a leader of your team, your business, or your community. Whether you've had kids or not, consider that your ultimate role in life is to elevate others, and most importantly, to make the world better for the next generation.

When you think from this expanded place, you will see that life becomes far more exciting and your path becomes clear.

Counterintuitive kids

If there is one skill I intentionally passed to my kids, it was how to be counterintuitive, and it started with focusing this lens on their role in life. Their journeys and success at such young ages show that counterintuitive thinking didn't just work for me, it worked for them. It will work for you and those who depend on you too.

I want to make clear that my kids' successes did not come from me funding their businesses or giving them roles in my companies. I would never want them to work for me because they would never experience the satisfaction that comes from creating a business themselves. True success can never be given; it must be earned. Instead, my focus was to prepare them with the counterintuitive skills they needed to find and seize their own opportunities.

Anu and I were very intentional about teaching our children to grow into adults who see situations from different perspectives—to be counterintuitive thinkers. When they were young, we reached a level of tremendous success when InfoSpace became one of the largest internet companies. During that time, we recognized that there was a high probability that our kids would grow up in an affluent home and become lazy as a result. We had seen this tragedy over and over with the kids of very successful people.

Anu and I were afraid of this fate for our kids, but we also didn't want to hold them back and make life as hard for them as it had once been for us. We recognized that our hard work and suffering had enabled us to give our kids greater opportunities than a school with a dirt floor. So, what we did was live by the principles that you will learn in this chapter. Here we'll explore ten counterintuitive ways of parenting (or leading and relating to others) that are also more broadly applicable in the quest to make the next generation great. In this chapter we'll cover the following topics:

1. Connecting dots

2. Make them hungry for truth and knowledge

3. They do what you do, not what you say

4. Exploration is everything

5. Love is unconditional, but pride is earned

6. Give them what's most valuable to you, not what's easy

7. Teach them to think beyond themselves

8. Don't make them learn the value of money the hard way

9. Redefine success as creating and learning to earn

10. Never use money to control people

Here's the other brilliant aspect of living your life with a focus on making the next generation great: To pass anything to the next generation, we have to do it ourselves. Any parent reading this will get this idea immediately. Once you become a parent you also start to think about the life you're living and how you behave. You want to be someone your children look up to. The same is true of leading in business—you want to leave a legacy of your values, culture, and goals that survives long beyond your own tenure.

1. Connecting dots

When my kids were young, our nighttime ritual was anything but ordinary. While many parents read stories to their children, which is a wonderful tradition, ours had a creative twist. Instead of reading to them, I asked our kids to tell me a story using three seemingly unrelated objects that I gave them. And then we'd reverse roles and they would ask me to tell them a story with three objects of their choice.

"Ankur, tell me a story about the ocean, a monkey, and a stone," I'd say. It was an activity designed to stretch their imagination and encourage them to find abstract connections between seemingly unrelated things.

Our storytelling ritual sparked some truly fascinating and hilarious tales. One night, Ankur and I imagined pirate monkeys scouring the oceans in search of a mystical stone that granted endless wishes. Another time, we conjured up astronaut pigs zooming through space seeking the most powerful dill pickle in the universe.

My kids would invite me to join in, and I'd spin a story using the random objects they chose. While this exercise is perfect for kids, I secretly found it just as beneficial. As adults, we often get caught up in logical, structured thinking. This exercise reminded me, again and again, how crucial it is to step outside the rigid boundaries of practical thinking and embrace imagination as the fuel that enables us to see situations from new perspectives and discover innovative solutions.

Since those wonderful years of sitting on the edge of their beds weaving stories, I have learned that many innovators of various eras have used similar techniques. Albert Einstein, for example, engaged in what he called combinatory play (yes, there's actually a term for the approach). He used various thinking exercises, such as pausing between focused bouts of scientific thinking around a problem to let his mind wander. This enabled him to make new and interesting connections. It's been said that this is how he formulated his famous equation, $E=MC^2$.

Leonardo da Vinci was a similar type of renaissance man who dabbled in multidisciplinary domains. He was an artist, inventor, scientist, and engineer and his wide range of interests allowed him to cross-pollinate ideas between disciplines, leading to innovative breakthroughs in both art and science. Leonardo is famous for painting the *Mona Lisa* and *The Last Supper*. He also dissected cadavers, contributed to the field of biology, and famously created the *Vitruvian Man*.

More recently, the world has seen multidisciplinary entrepreneurs succeed. Steve Jobs, for example, credited a calligraphy class he took in college as the inspiration for the typography that became central to Apple's design.

If you can imagine it, you have a shot at achieving it. And connecting dots is critical to seeing paths that make the impossible possible. This is also how you encourage others to enjoy the process of thinking and the pursuit of solutions to problems. It's how you make them *hungry*.

2. Make them hungry for truth and knowledge

The primary role of a leader or parent isn't to force-feed others' intellects. It is to make them hungry for truth and knowledge. And what drives this hunger? Intellectual curiosity.

Intellectual curiosity is the drive to ask, "What if?" and "Why?" Once this curiosity is sparked, it becomes an unquenchable desire—a constant need to learn. A curious mind is a critical aspect of being counterintuitive.

This is why you should never rush to give someone a solution or advice without first asking them to reflect. The way to be someone who sparks curiosity in others is by *asking questions that get them to think*. Too often I see parents, coaches, and business leaders *giving* people the answers. Instead, we have to convince them to *think*, because people learn when they have to struggle and reach conclusions for themselves.

Next time a child says to you, "Look at the beautiful blue sky!" try challenging them with a question like, "What do you think the sky is made of? Why can't you put some in a bucket and take it home? If it's really blue, why doesn't it stain your skin?"

With questions like this you can show that even 'truths' they take for granted might be different than they assume. From there you can go deeper. What if the sky doesn't exist as they think it does? What if the blue they see up there is simply how their mind interprets light, since color itself is something created within our brains?

Questions are what provoke and inspire young minds to challenge assumptions and see the world with fresh eyes. Ultimately, this leads to minds that create, solve impossible feats, and drive remarkable results.

In order to get others to be curious, you have to be an intellectually curious person yourself. So, use your imagination to be curious about ideas first and foremost. Always ask "Why?" Never immediately accept any idea. Engage in wonder like you did when you were a child. It's as important (or even more important) for adults as for kids, and for leaders as for those they lead. If you do this constantly, it's easy for you to help others do the same.

To encourage this approach, you might find it helpful to introduce curiosity practices. When I founded my first company, I aimed to challenge the traditional corporate, business-school mindset around work. To encourage innovation, I introduced the '30-Minute Rule,' where any employee, regardless of rank, could take 30 minutes during the workday to explore a new idea for a feature or product. After dedicating just 30 minutes to researching and experimenting, they would usually gain a clear sense of the potential challenges and opportunities. This approach helped me quickly evaluate whether an idea was worth pursuing further with the team.

Every idea, no matter how ridiculous it sounded, was always given 30 minutes. It was a key part of our product development, but also a great way to teach the employees to think like entrepreneurs. When your employees start thinking of themselves as having a hand in the direction of the company, and being their own individual research and development micro-lab, they produce much better work.

The quick-hit nature of the rule was quintessentially entrepreneurial. I've never believed in business plans, because you can never fully anticipate all the factors which will contribute to the success or failure of a business idea. This is simply one method I deployed, but you can do all sorts of things to spark curiosity. Now, whatever you do, never forget that the most important way to help others be curious is to be curious yourself, which brings us to the next principle.

3. They do what you do, not what you say

When our kids were still young, I reached a crossroads: I could sell my business and retire or start another venture. The idea of taking time off crossed my mind, but I caught myself. What would my kids see? A dad lounging at home telling them, "Work hard if you want to succeed" while they trudge off to school every day?

It's a common scenario: a person achieves financial success and thinks, "I'll quit and spend more time at home with my young kids." Sounds great, right? But that decision can be one of the most self-centered choices you can make. It can harm your kids more than it helps them. Imagine it from the perspective of your children. Mom or Dad only worked hard to make money. After that, they chose to spend their days sitting on the couch watching CNBC. What's the takeaway for the kids? "I am already growing up in an affluent family and I want to grow up just like my dad, so I can lay on the couch and watch CNBC." It sets a precedent that success means working hard for money and then coasting. That's not the message most of us want to pass down, whether it's to our kids or to the next generation of business leaders. We want to inspire creative thinking, innovation, and ambition.

So I chose to start a second company, and then a third. Each successive company was more and more audacious. My kids were in their teens when I started Moon Express, and young adults when I founded Viome. They have watched it all and have learned that they, too, can give themselves permission to tackle the world's toughest challenges. All they need is the willingness to try and the counterintuitive skills to produce results.

Almost every kid thinks that they are smarter than their parents, and most young employees seem to think they're smarter than their boss. So, if they see you take on and overcome an audacious challenge, they assume that they can achieve even greater things.

The most powerful way to show others what works is with your actions. So, should you leave work and go home and spend time with your children? No. Don't fall into that trap. Let them watch you work hard and succeed.

The same is true in the workplace. Others understand you from your actions and behaviors, not necessarily from what you say. Many people and organizations claim to have values but act in a way completely contrary to those values.

In short, in all walks of life, lead by example.

4. Exploration is everything

When my daughter Priyanka was 16, she came to me and said, "Dad, I know you love science and technology, but the passion I want to pursue is not anything to do with those things."

Though I was happy to learn that Priyanka had found something she felt so strongly about, I also realized that I hadn't done part of my job as a parent—I hadn't helped her explore the vast range of opportunities the world offers, beyond my own focus on science and technology.

At 16, it was too early for her to have a passion. One critical role of a parent (or leader) is about exposure. So, I told Priyanka I would love for her to go to Singularity University, where she could learn about nanotechnology, biotechnology, robotics, artificial intelligence, supercomputing, and how they can be used to solve pressing global challenges. Priyanka wasn't impressed. "Dad, you didn't hear a word I said. I just told you I don't like science and technology."

I asked her how she could claim she didn't like something if she had no experience with it. So, we made a deal. I told her that if she went with an open mind, genuinely wanting to learn she could come back and choose her own path, and I'd fully support her.

That summer, Priyanka went to Singularity University. When she returned, she said, "Dad, I've made up my mind." I was a little nervous about this, but I said, "All right, tell me what you want—it's your decision."

She looked at me with a deadpan expression and said, "I want to be a geneticist or a neuroscientist." I was stunned.

"My dear, what happened?" I asked.

Priyanka said that before she went to Singularity University she had thought science and technology had no connection to her interests. Yet, after opening her mind she found that science and technology are tools that would help her to follow her passion, which was (and still is) women's health.

Reflect on that for a moment. What if I hadn't challenged Priyanka to attend Singularity University and had supported her decision to avoid science? She might never have been exposed to new ideas and never have discovered her true calling.

Her first mission after graduating from Stanford was to use artificial intelligence to remove gender bias in hiring. Now she runs Evvy biosciences, a women's health company filling the gender health gap using genetics and artificial intelligence. What if I had done what many parents might have done? The world would have lost out on a great entrepreneur who is now making a real difference in women's lives, and Priyanka may not have really succeeded with her true passion to help girls and women around the world.

So many people grow up deciding too early what to do with their lives and without fully understanding the tools available, or, more importantly, how they can truly succeed in making their passion successful. Exposing yourself and others constantly to diverse ideas, thoughts, and experiences is crucial to discovering any purpose and realizing it. Instead of rushing to specialize, it's valuable to explore widely.

But, of course, for them to be explorers, you have to build an environment around them where they feel safe to try new endeavors, go on adventures, and take risks.

5. Love is unconditional, but pride is earned

My kids had a very different upbringing than I did. While my parents struggled with poverty, my children grew up in an affluent household. My success with InfoSpace provided them with a life of abundance. And so, when they were very young, Anu and I were concerned. We worried they might lack motivation because their lives were so comfortable. We asked ourselves how we could instill the right values and a strong work ethic.

Ultimately, we realized it was possible to give them a solid foundation while fostering curiosity, engagement, and a genuine drive for life. We always told our kids that our love for them was unconditional, but our approval was not. We would say, "We love you and will always love you, but we won't just tell you that we are proud of you unless you do things that *make us* proud of you."

Children need to know that they have a safe and loving place at home, which means that your love for them has to be unconditional. A child needs to understand that there is nothing they can do to not be loved by you. As your offspring they need to know that they are central to you and that love is a given. They can make mistakes but your love for them doesn't waiver. Although you hope that they will always learn from every mistake they make, there are times they won't.

But that doesn't mean you'll always be proud of them.

Pride and love are two different gifts every person can give to another, and they should be defined and distinct.

When a person knows they have your love, they feel safe enough to explore the world. In that safety, they can be themselves, and even discover who they are. Mistakes are inevitable, but with the right support, those missteps become lessons. And through continued exploration, new ideas emerge, some of which may one day lead to real breakthroughs.

Of course, 'love' is more appropriate in parenting than in the workplace, but this still translates to offering nurturing support for creative exploration and respecting your team's right to make and learn from mistakes.

It's important to connect pride with the right qualities and goals. Our kids knew we were proud when they improved the lives of people around them, solved problems, and explored new ideas. As young kids do, they would shrug and say: "Whatever, Dad." But, decades later, each of them remembers the little chats we had that helped them take actions to make us, their parents, proud.

Over the years, I have watched my kids do incredible things, and I am incredibly proud of the work they've done to improve lives. They found big problems and they realized they could go out and solve these problems. Why do they all share this same mindset? Because they were always loved and supported, so *they felt safe to explore and create*, but they only earned admiration when they did things that were truly deserving of genuine pride.

6. Give them what's most valuable to you, not what's easy

Most successful people lead busy lives and often feel guilty about not spending enough time with their children. To ease that guilt, many resort to showering their kids with expensive gifts and fulfilling their every desire. It's easy to use money because they can always earn more. But what their children truly need is their presence, not just when it's convenient for the parents, but when the kids need them most. Time, not money, is the most valuable gift a parent can give.

I made a simple rule; it's one I never break and one you might want to adopt: No matter what I'm doing, if my kids call, I take the call. No exceptions. They know I will always be available to them whenever they need me. Their calls are set to bypass 'Do Not Disturb' so they can reach me under any circumstances. Once, while speaking at a Goldman Sachs conference to an audience of a few hundred top portfolio managers, my phone rang—it was Ankur. I paused, excused myself, and said, "I'm sorry, it's my son. I promised him I'd always answer his calls, so I have to take this." I checked that he was okay then asked to call him back. The exchange only lasted a few seconds, then I resumed my speech.

The impact was profound. Our stock jumped massively after I took the call. Why? Because everyone listening learned that I was a man who keeps the promises I make, regardless of the circumstances. They saw someone with unshakeable priorities, and that inspired trust.

Simple, unwavering commitments like this one make a difference. Your children need to know that they can reach you when they need to—that's part of loving them. If they don't have a basis and foundation of safety, they will not feel safe to explore the world and learn, which is what you want them to do.

My commitment has always been to show them that I'm willing to give them what's most valuable to me—my time and attention—whenever they need it.

7. Teach them to think beyond themselves

Anu and I didn't want our kids to grow up self-indulgent or self-centered, so we came up with a plan. When each of our children turned ten, we encouraged them to research charities and support a cause they cared deeply about. With our guidance, they learned how they could raise funds and spread awareness about their cause. One of the ways they achieved this was by asking friends and family to donate to their chosen charity instead of giving them birthday gifts.

Priyanka became so invested in her support for young girls in India that she flew there to visit the remote villages that would benefit from her work. That experience transformed her perspective. Instead of spending money on expensive clothes, she began to prioritize helping others meet their basic needs. She no longer saw herself in isolation but as part of a larger society, with a responsibility to contribute as a compassionate human being.

The goal was twofold: first, to help the children develop the skills they would need as adults to become successful entrepreneurs, and second, to encourage them to focus on something greater than their own immediate pleasure. Instead of spending money on drinks and parties, they started thinking about how they could save and direct those resources to their charitable work. Their entire mindset shifted—they found joy not just in personal gratification but in the happiness of helping others.

This simple exercise kept them grounded through high school and college, steering them away from trouble and keeping their focus on making a positive impact. In time, they came to realize that they could build businesses that do immense good for the world while also achieving financial success.

Though they don't always expect to, everyone feels better about their life when they think beyond themselves in an effort to help others. Encourage this line of thinking no matter who you are leading. In business you can start by opening up opportunities for experienced staff to onboard, train, and mentor new starters, or support time off to contribute to charitable causes. Simple things like this foster an environment of expansive, outward-focused thought. Who knows where it might lead?

8. Don't make them learn the value of money the hard way

Most people have to work hard to earn money, unless they inherit generational wealth. When they have children, they often want their kids to experience the same struggles they did, believing it will be good for their growth.

It's common for parents to teach their children the value of money to prevent them from becoming entitled. Many encourage their kids to take jobs at grocery stores or fast-food restaurants to understand what it takes to earn a dollar. In a way, they want their children to endure the same hardships they faced. But imposing that struggle on them simply because we endured it ourselves is a traditional, outdated approach. We can do much better if we apply counterintuitive thinking.

Instead of asking our kids to work summer jobs just to earn money, we encouraged them to spend their summers learning about subjects they were passionate about—topics they didn't have time to explore during the school year. This meant pursuing unpaid internships to gain practical knowledge in fields that genuinely interested them. Our youngest chose to study the human brain at the Allen Institute for Brain Science, while our daughter explored how babies' brains develop at the University of Washington.

Our kids didn't start from where we did, and we chose to honor that. Rather than making them begin at square one, we gave them the benefit of the platform we built as a family. Our goal wasn't for them to simply surpass us by a small margin, but to use what we've accomplished as a launch pad—so they can shoot for the stars.

Hopefully you'll reach a point of abundance in your business, in which case I encourage you to lead from the position you're currently in, not from the position at which you started. If cash is readily available, don't pay your staff as if it pains you to see every dollar go. If you once had to hustle 24/7 to stay afloat but now you can take Fridays off and still turn a profit, don't inflict the past trauma on today's workplace.

9. Redefine success as creating and learning to earn

We always encouraged our kids not to measure success by how much money they had in the bank but by *how many lives they improved*. Once you redefine success in this way, life becomes a game of contribution. I still share this lesson with every young leader I encounter. *Making money is a byproduct of improving lives.*

Ownership without creation often leads to stagnation and a lack of contribution. If someone hasn't created anything meaningful, but owns a lot, they risk becoming a drain on society.

Consider children who come from wealthy families. Despite their access to immense resources, if they don't engage in creation or meaningful contribution, they fail to give back to humanity in any significant way. This lack of purpose and contribution often deprives them of true satisfaction and joy, leaving them unfulfilled.

I knew that the more lives my kids improved, the bigger the company they would get to create. If you don't teach this to kids, they are likely to focus on chasing money, which might lead to financial abundance but not deep fulfillment and success. Instead, my approach gets you both.

Using your intellect and skill is the best way to generate money. Success is about orienting yourself to obsessions you want to pursue and solving problems that others need solved. We always focused on helping our kids find areas and topics they wanted to learn about and explore.

If you improve life for a large group of people or use your intellect to transform an industry or field, money is simple. Don't be a parasite and don't inspire anyone around you to be one either. Business and life are about learning, creating, and making humanity better. Money is a natural byproduct.

The work of my kids proves my point. These days, they even remind me of lessons I once taught them and teach me new ways to run a business. Nothing makes me prouder than when those three succeed, because they are living lives they love and making a massive positive impact on society. The best way to make this happen is to be someone who sparks curiosity, who makes others think. This is the greatest achievement a parent or leader can hope for.

10. Never use money to control

A lot of parents remind kids that they can spend their money the way they want when they earn it themselves. They tell their kids if they want to do the summer program abroad then they need to earn money to do it.

But if children grow up believing that the only way to have freedom or get what they want is to make lots of money then they spend their lives chasing money. We want our kids to focus on tackling audacious challenges that can positively impact billions of people around the world, not go chasing quick money-making schemes. A pay check isn't everything in the workplace, either (though it is important). Find other ways that incentivize impactful activities. There's a reason that Employee of the Month status is awarded in so many businesses.

In our family, we also focused on spending money if the entire family agreed it was the right thing to do. This allowed kids to learn to manage money from a place of smart decision making and impact. We always looked at success as a team effort, a 'family success.' There was never a discussion about *our* money and *their* money. It was all about what was the right thing to do. We did this to encourage them to focus on being responsible with money, use it on learning and experiences that enrich their lives, and to do tremendous good for humanity.

Remember, you're part of an eight-billion-person family

Everyone has a biological family defined by shared DNA. For many, these are the people who raise and shape them through love, teaching, and guidance. But family is not always defined by biology. For others, similar bonds are created by shared experiences, mutual trust, and genuine care.

On a larger scale, humanity itself functions as a kind of family. From a genetic perspective, all humans are remarkably similar, sharing 99% of the same DNA. Yet humanity is also connected not by personal relationships but by a shared history. Our ancestors created the societies, knowledge, and systems that support our lives today. Every road we travel, every piece of technology we use, and every institution we depend on is part of this inherited legacy.

Being part of humanity's family comes with responsibility. What are you doing to contribute to this collective effort? Are you building something that benefits others, whether through work, community involvement, or ideas? Are you raising future generations or inspiring the next wave of business talent to think critically and act with integrity? Are your actions creating opportunities for others to thrive?

These are not abstract questions; they shape the reality we live in. Each of us makes choices that influence the larger human story. Take a moment to consider how your actions today reflect your role in this shared family. What steps can you take to strengthen it, and how can you encourage others to do the same? Who do you want to be and what do you want to do? Whatever your answer, you need to ensure you are in a fit state to carry out these duties, particularly if you're committing to the long term. So next we'll turn our counterintuitive lens onto the topic of health and wellbeing.

Conventional thought trap

Many parents believe their role is to teach their children values, help them excel academically, and secure a fulfilling job in the established workplace. The leaders in that workplace then pick up the baton, applying very narrow thinking to define success.

But this traditional thinking is limited, and reinforces the fallacy that money comes first and success follows.

Counterintuitive approach

Your primary job is to teach your kids (and those you lead) to be *intellectually curious* and to focus on meaningful goals that improve lives, with money following as a byproduct. The same goes for employees. This is achieved by leading by example, exposure to new environments, and instilling the right values.

Focus on improving lives, learning, and staying curious. From this focus, financial abundance, great relationships, and deep fulfillment are natural outputs.

CHAPTER 7

COUNTERINTUITIVE HEALTH

"To keep the body in good health is a duty... otherwise we shall not be able to keep our mind strong and clear."

—Buddha

IN 2013, MY dad was diagnosed with prostate cancer. He survived it. But then just a year later, he faced another life-threatening condition. He suffered a heart aneurysm while walking up a hill. This too, he survived. But I couldn't help but notice the toll these events took on his body.

At the time, I was in my 50s and beginning to feel the effects of aging myself. I had a little extra weight around my waist, and my energy was fading bit by bit. Watching my father's health struggles made me consider my own future. Would my body fail me too? Would I reach a point where I could no longer do the things I loved?

It's a trajectory we're taught to expect. As we age, our health declines. Most of us realize too late just how important staying healthy is, wishing we'd prioritized it earlier. So, I decided to make some changes.

I started walking more, chose healthier foods, and thought deeply about my future.

At the same time, I reflected on my family history. My dad's mother lived healthily until the age of 99, and his father reached 100. Yet my dad seemed to have broken this family mold. Why? And how could I avoid the same fate? How could I keep my body healthy and thriving as long as possible and be able to do what I want to do?

Around this time, Moon Express was booming. We had recently secured the company's ownership rights to anything we brought back from the Moon (rather than those rights falling to any nation), an essential part of our business model. Concerned about my health, I briefly considered retirement, but realized that without a purpose my mind and body would likely deteriorate. I'd seen it happen to others, including my father. After retiring from his government job, he seemed to lose his enthusiasm for life, and with it, his health began to decline further. That's when I began to question what I could dedicate the next decade of my life to. The answer was right in front of me: The challenge of aging and chronic disease.

I didn't want to follow the same path as so many others, falling victim to preventable illnesses. I knew it was possible to avoid them. After all, there are 90-year-old triathletes proving what the human body is capable of. Some people manage to keep their bodies biologically younger than their chronological age, enjoying vibrant health well into their 90s and beyond.

With this realization, I launched Viome, a mission to combat chronic disease and the decline caused by aging. Over the next three years, I delved deeply into cutting-edge health science, built connections with world-renowned experts, and became a test subject for emerging health technologies. My own health metrics improved, and I felt optimistic about the future, confident that I could take control of my health. I became biologically younger and fitter even as I aged chronologically. But in the midst of this transformative journey, I received a devastating call: my dad had been diagnosed with stage four pancreatic cancer.

Pancreatic cancer is a silent killer. It is notoriously difficult to detect until it's too late. My dad had been complaining about stomach pain, but his doctor initially dismissed it as something minor. He was told to take antacids. When the pain persisted, my dad was sent for an MRI and our worst fears were confirmed.

Watching him undergo chemotherapy was devastating. He lost weight, his hair fell out, and he became a different person. Watching him decline was difficult, but it reminded me of the principle that if we don't have our health, we have nothing. Declining health is not something I want to experience myself. Nor do I want the people I love, or, frankly, anyone in this world to go through it.

As I built Viome, I gained invaluable insights into human health. We made significant progress in our moonshot goal of making aging and illness optional. Yet, the business was still in its early stages, and despite all I had learned, I could not save my father. Desperate, I delved into research and discovered studies highlighting innovative treatments. I pleaded with his oncologist to try an experimental approach but he declined, adhering strictly to the standard protocol. A few months later, my dad passed away.

I realized the limitations of traditional medicine and the importance of taking personal responsibility for understanding our bodies and managing our health before it takes control of us. Much like a negative mindset, an unhealthy body can hold you back from fully engaging in life and make achieving success difficult.

Before my father died, I said to him, "Dad, I couldn't save you, but I won't stop until we find a way to end chronic diseases."

His death was a turning point for me, cementing my commitment to my moonshot. And throughout this latest journey with Viome, if there is one thing I've never been more certain of it is that health *is* wealth.

Confucius once said: "A healthy man has a thousand wishes; a sick man only has one." His words couldn't ring truer.

Without health, everything else loses its value. When you're healthy, you have the energy to pursue your passions, the strength to turn ideas into reality, and the clarity to make the most of your time. Yet, so many of us take our health for granted, prioritizing work, convenience, and short-term goals over long-term well-being. Neglecting health seems harmless at first. We skip workouts here and there. We sacrifice sleep. We eat a few sugary foods and think it's nothing. Small, unhealthy choices can accumulate over time, and by the time the consequences become apparent, reversing the damage becomes significantly more challenging.

Isn't it mindboggling that when we are young, we often sacrifice our health to achieve wealth, only to sacrifice our wealth to get our health back as we age. In the process we lose out on all the enjoyments we could have had if we maintained good health to begin with.

And so, once again, acting counterintuitively is the panacea. Even if we feel healthy, we must focus on wellness to ensure that our health is a priority.

Over the course of my Viome journey, I have also learned to bring counterintuitive thinking to my health to optimize it and even reverse aging. As I've questioned my own thinking and taken new actions, my health continues to improve year by year. Now in my 60s, I run up hills and take two stairs at a time. And I have found a way to seamlessly integrate health practices into my life.

We live in a time where technology and tools make achieving and maintaining good health more attainable than ever. Yet, to fully embrace these advances, most people need to first shift their mindset and belief system about health. I know this journey well because I've walked it myself. When I started Viome, I wasn't a health enthusiast—I was simply curious. But as I delved into cutting-edge science, I uncovered and debunked countless myths I had once believed about health. Now, I understand why so many struggle to take the first step: the true foundation for better health isn't just access to tools—it's a transformation in how we think about our well-being.

The good news is that science and technology are rapidly advancing, making it easier than ever to take control of our health. Today, we understand more about the importance of the gut microbiome, the role of inflammation in chronic disease, and the power of lifestyle choices. Small, consistent actions have a profound impact on our biological health.

Through Viome, I'm working to make these tools accessible to everyone, so we can create a future where chronic disease is optional. Losing my father reminded me just how fragile our bodies are and how crucial it is to care for them. His passing ignited a fire in me to push harder, dream bigger, and ensure that fewer families have to endure the pain of preventable illness.

Health is wealth. Without it, we have nothing. But with it, we have the power to achieve the impossible. And that's a lesson I'll carry with me for the rest of my life. My goal here is to get you to see that having the vitality and body of a 30-year-old is possible into your nineties and beyond.

Deprioritizing the most important priority

I'm sure you have experienced a time when you were ill and had to stop everything. Suddenly, and often without warning, you get sick and you can't go to work, take the dog for a walk, or sit at the dinner table with the family.

It's very likely that you have had it much worse. If you have had to live with a chronic disease for a long period of time, health is likely a particularly high priority for you. If that's the case, I'm certain that the 'health is wealth' principle is one you understand well.

It's easy to put health on the back burner, isn't it? Even when we care about it, the unhealthy influences around us make it hard. It feels like we're trying to stay healthy but facing obstacles every single day, from our environment, to cultural beauty ideals, to foods and products ladened with toxins, and more.

There are so many variables against us that we can bucket them into two categories:

1. Your biology

2. Your environment

These are factors you probably have a great deal of experience with. Let me briefly touch on them before talking about how to overcome them.

Barrier 1: Your biology

When it comes to health, it may seem like your own body works against you.

The human body evolved to seek out high-calorie foods as a survival mechanism during times of scarcity. In today's world of abundance, this instinct often leads to overeating and weight gain. Similarly, our natural drive to conserve energy, once essential for survival, now contributes to sedentary lifestyles that can result in obesity and heart disease. Additionally, stress responses that once protected us in life-threatening situations such as running away from a chasing tiger now continuously being activated in response to everyday challenges—like a demanding boss or a nagging spouse—lead to prolonged cortisol release, which can cause high blood pressure, weakened immunity, and weight gain.

The human brain naturally prioritizes short-term gratification, seeking immediate pleasure over long-term benefits. This explains why you might reach for a chocolate bar instead of an apple—it's quick, satisfying, and provides an instant energy boost. It also tends to focus on immediate demands while overlooking long-term risks, a behavior rooted in survival instincts. For example, you might skip lunch to finish a project, putting the task ahead of your body's needs. And when your cells are low on energy, your body pushes you toward quick fixes, like the chocolate bar, to refuel.

Even when we want to take a break, social pressures can make it harder. If colleagues aren't taking lunch breaks, the social environment adds another obstacle to prioritizing health.

Barrier 2: Your environment

Modern life is full of obstacles that make prioritizing health increasingly difficult. The industrial era has created a world dominated by processed foods, chemical-laden products, and nutrient-depleted crops—all of which contribute to chronic health issues. Compounding this is a healthcare system designed to treat symptoms rather than address root causes, an outdated framework poorly equipped to handle today's chronic disease epidemic.

Society's glorification of productivity leaves little time for self-care, while structural challenges like limited time, financial constraints, and unequal access to resources further hinder well-being. Social pressures also play a significant role—when those around us make unhealthy choices, we're likely to follow, reinforcing cycles of poor habits.

Even for those striving to make healthier choices, misinformation and fleeting health fads can lead to confusion and frustration. Cultural beauty standards add another layer of distraction, prioritizing appearance over true well-being in pursuit of social validation.

These factors combine to create an environment that not only fails to support health but often actively works against it, making the pursuit of well-being a daunting challenge in today's world.

But there is good news too. Despite these challenges, we are in a unique moment of opportunity. Never before have we had access to such advanced tools, extensive scientific knowledge, and abundant data to understand what true health looks like. Affordable technology, deeper science, and more precise data allow us to uncover what works and what doesn't, paving the way for a better approach to health.

The greatest hurdle, however, is that most people don't realize what they're missing. True health begins with the right mindset. By adopting a smarter, more intentional approach, prioritizing well-being becomes second nature, unlocking the full potential of a healthy body.

This shift requires seeing yourself not as a passive follower waiting for advice, but as the CEO of your own health. It starts with recognizing that you are biologically unique—biochemically distinct from anyone else. To thrive, you must understand your body's needs and respond to them in real time. The more attuned you become to giving your body exactly what it needs, the healthier you will be.

Becoming the CEO of your body

Just a few decades back, it was common for doctors to withhold a terminal cancer diagnosis from a patient if they believed it was in the patient's best interest. Physicians often felt that allowing the patient to enjoy their final months without the burden of understanding the severity of their condition was preferable to focusing on their impending death. This could lead to some very traumatizing revelations for the patient and their family during their last days together.

This was part of a medical model known as 'paternalism,' where doctors held the authority over medical information, diagnoses, and treatment decisions. It left patients with little agency in their own healthcare, relying entirely on their doctors' judgment.

The field of medicine was viewed as a near-sacred calling. Doctors were regarded as trusted authorities whose primary role was to make the best decisions for their patients. However, the lack of transparency also led to confusion, a lack of trust, and, ultimately, a passive role for patients in managing their own health.

By the 1970s, a shift toward patient-centered care had begun. Informed consent, shared decision-making, and full disclosure of medical information became commonplace. Patients were considered partners in their healthcare, entitled to understand their health status, ask questions, and make choices in line with their values and priorities.

It's ironic to think that we are all born with a body, yet for much of history—and even to some extent today—we've been poorly equipped to understand how to care for it. Thankfully, it is now considered unethical for doctors to withhold health information from patients. However, the medical system and physicians still hold significant authority over healthcare decisions, and many people continue to rely too heavily on doctors as all-knowing authorities on health.

We are entering an exciting era of precision medicine, a transformative shift toward a future where individuals have greater control, knowledge, and freedom to make informed decisions about their health. Advances in technology are making healthcare tools more affordable and accessible, leading to an unprecedented democratization of health knowledge. This empowers you to own your health data, understand your body's unique needs, and take charge of your health journey like never before.

This shift requires a new approach, and because we are transitioning from one era to the next, the steps to achieve your healthiest self might feel counterintuitive. In the past, it was common to wait for guidance and rely solely on doctors, as tools to access information about our bodies simply didn't exist. That's no longer the case. Those who recognize this shift and embrace the available tools and knowledge are at a distinct advantage, giving them the opportunity to live their healthiest lives.

There are three critical practices to engage if you want to experience your healthiest life:

1. Measure your metrics

How does a CEO know if a business is successful or failing? What's their scorecard? They look at profits and losses. They look at dollars and cents and spreadsheets of numbers to know how to improve and grow. Similarly, to be the CEO of your body, you must track and know your biometrics. Only then will you have a baseline to work from, fully immersed in the day-to-day reality of your health.

Just like in business, metrics can help you assess where you stand— whether it's your position in the market or, in the case of health, your biological measures compared to averages. These benchmarks provide valuable context for understanding what is considered healthy and what isn't. To make the most of this, you need to adopt a second key practice: gaining a basic understanding of human biology. Staying informed about the latest scientific advancements is crucial for making better decisions and improving your health.

2. Understand emerging science

Collecting data on your body is only useful if you have the context to interpret it. Without that, the data lacks meaning. Without an understanding of what is scientifically proven to be healthy, you remain at a disadvantage when it comes to making informed decisions about how to maintain your health.

Just as an effective CEO benefits from a broad understanding of how to run a business, you need a foundational knowledge of health to make informed decisions. A basic understanding of scientifically proven facts can also help you avoid falling victim to misinformation. Many common pitfalls in health stem from outdated beliefs or practices, which I will expand on shortly. The key takeaway here is that understanding basic biological science is essential for taking smart, effective actions toward better health.

3. Oversee and tend to the five areas

Like a CEO who runs a business with multiple divisions, you have five areas to oversee when it comes to health:

1. Purpose
2. Sleep
3. Fitness
4. Stress
5. Nutrition

If you want to stay in shape you have to make these areas that contribute to your health a constant focus.

Unfortunately, unlike a CEO, you can't hire anyone to do the work for you. No, you can't outsource your squats! That is on you. However, I've developed a framework to help you strategically prioritize key areas of your health and integrate them into your lifestyle. The more you build habits related to these areas, keep them in check, and improve them, the better you'll be at avoiding illness and the decline often associated with aging.

Now, let's dive into these three practices in a deeper way.

Practice 1: Measure your metrics

In business, there's a well-known adage: 'Measure what matters.' This means tracking metrics like revenue, expenses, and customer satisfaction to ensure growth and success. The same principle applies to health—measuring what matters is crucial. Tracking actual data, rather than relying on assumptions or hypothetical ideas, makes it much easier to understand your progress and make informed decisions.

We are entering the era of precision medicine, a field that has only recently emerged, making it easier than ever to know what steps to take to stay healthy and maintain peak performance. To grasp the significance of this moment in health, it's helpful to compare it to the evolution of computers, which followed a similar path of rapid progression and accessibility.

The first computers were massive, room-sized machines that required specialized knowledge to operate. If a company had a mainframe computer, employees had to rely on experts to run it, as they controlled access to the information. Over time, as technology advanced and components became more affordable, computers became smaller, more powerful, and easier for non-specialists to use. Eventually, personal computers emerged, allowing ordinary people to access information from their desks—whether at work or at home. A tool once reserved for experts became widely available, empowering individuals in unprecedented ways. Today, we carry powerful computers in our pockets, connecting us to the world's knowledge and equipping us with an array of tracking and productivity tools.

A similar transformation is happening in healthcare. As diagnostic and tracking tools have become more affordable and accessible, individuals can monitor and understand their health metrics. Finally, we are empowered to take charge of our well-being because we have access to scientific information and tools that we never had before. At the same time, this scientific information and these tools are advancing at an accelerated rate because technology grows exponentially.

The bottom line is that we can now access information about our bodies in order to make smart decisions and prevent decline.

Therefore, if you want to stay healthy, your first step is to take advantage of the tools available today to measure your metrics. If you don't track your metrics, you don't know what to change. Important biometrics to track are:

- Weight

- Muscle mass

- Bone density

- Physical activity

- Sleep time and quality

- Heart rate variability (HRV)

- Blood glucose levels

- Hormones

- Toxicity levels

To measure health matters correctly, you need to know and stay on top of what tools are available.

Already, millions of people are choosing to take control of their health by monitoring their metrics with wearable devices and apps. There are also numerous affordable, personalized at-home test kits that provide data on microbiome and cellular health. With semi-annual affordable tests you can gather the data points you need to make informed health choices and stay healthy. There are six tests I recommend you do to cover all of the biometrics mentioned here, but new and improved technologies are always emerging, so it is important to remain informed. Here is a summary so you know what's available:

Metatranscriptomics microbiome tests

Viome is the only company that offers these advanced, at-home tests. They provide a comprehensive analysis of gene expression data from all organisms in a sample, as well as their functions and interactions with the host's immune system. From this data they are able to predict whether you are moving towards a disease state or moving away from a disease state. They can also reveal which pre-disease states are forming in the body at a molecular level, so we can get ahead of them. The Full Body Intelligence Test also includes data on cellular health.

Body composition scans

For affordable and accessible body scans, consider a DEXA scan. This scan measures bone density and body composition, helping to assess risks for osteoporosis and fractures. It also provides insights into body fat and muscle mass, including the distribution of fat in different areas of your body.

If you're looking for a more advanced option, the AMRA BCP scan is worth considering. This scan uses MRI technology to provide detailed measurements of fat and muscle volumes. Approved in the U.S. in 2020, it is available at select MRI centers. However, it is a more expensive option compared to a DEXA scan.

Toxicity tests

These tests are valuable for identifying harmful substances in the body, such as heavy metals and mycotoxins. Heavy metal tests measure blood levels of metals like lead and mercury, which can enter the body through environmental exposure or diet. Mycotoxin tests detect harmful mold metabolites associated with conditions like kidney toxicity, immune suppression, and neurotoxicity.

Hormone tests

Hormonal imbalances, which can be identified through these tests, often reveal issues within the body's glands. Hormones are critical for regulating various functions, including growth, mood, stress response, metabolism, and sexual health, among other essential systems.

Food sensitivity tests

There are a variety of tests on the market that offer insights into which foods may be causing negative symptoms.

Nutrition metabolite tests

These tests analyze substances produced by a person's metabolism. They show how well your body is using nutrients.

All these tests, except for the DEXA scan, use an at-home collection kit to collect biological samples, which are sent for analysis to a lab.

Anyone who's serious about health should also regularly monitor standard blood biomarkers, such as HbA1c, apoB, and hsCRP. Many tests performed in annual health checks, such as HbA1c, should be done more frequently, every three-to-six months, depending on your health status. And there are many other tests you should take that are not included in a standard physical, such as homocysteine, uric acid, and lp(a), among others.

While many experts predict the hospitals of the future will be in our homes, we are already seeing an early version of this trend today using these kits. Millions of people are already taking advantage of these tests (and other affordable health tools like wearable devices and trackers) to achieve better health outcomes, and they will lead to greater longevity rates.

Once you have the metrics, the next step is understanding how to use them to take meaningful action. The key question to ask yourself is: "If this is where I am, and that's where I want to be, what steps do I need to take to get from here to there?" Staying up to date with the latest science is crucial for answering this effectively.

Take building muscle as an example. You know that strength training and a higher protein intake are essential, but the first step is tracking your current muscle mass to establish a baseline. From there, treat it as a process of experimentation. Commit to specific actions, like following a workout plan or adjusting your diet, and track your progress regularly. These measurements will show whether your approach is working. If the results aren't what you expect, it's a signal to seek new information, refine your strategy, and make adjustments to optimize your outcomes. This ongoing cycle of action, measurement, and adaptation is the key to achieving your goals.

Success in this process requires a solid understanding of basic biology and the latest advancements in health science. Let's take a look at this now.

Practice 2: Understand emerging science

Launching Viome has completely transformed my perspective on health and reshaped my body, along with my outlook on life. Delving into the data, collaborating with experts, and exploring cutting-edge science has been an extraordinary and eye-opening journey.

Before all this, I believed many myths about health that I now realize were shaped by outdated knowledge. These beliefs, rooted in the past, are the same obstacles that hold most people back today. I explore these and others in depth in my book, *The Youth Formula*, where I delve into the science behind them. If you've read the book, you're already ahead of the curve. If not, I revisit the two most common myths here to highlight their significance and demonstrate how they impact your health choices.

It's easy to fall back into old patterns or be influenced by those who still hold onto outdated ideas. However, by understanding and embracing the latest science, you can break free from these misconceptions and take control of your health.

Myth 1: DNA determines health trajectory

Like most people, I once looked at my parents to get an idea of what would be my fate as I aged. And if I got sick or gained a few pounds, I blamed my genetics. As many people do, I'd say, "It's in our family!" But then I learned the truth, that the blueprint in your cells—your DNA—does not predict health or longevity in the way we once assumed.

Your DNA isn't a crystal ball for predicting your health or lifespan. It shows what's *possible* but not what's actually *happening* in your body. Every cell in our body has the same DNA, but not every cell behaves the same way. For instance, our eyes, skin, and heart cells are all unique because different parts of the DNA are active in each. This is why we don't have eyes growing on our hands and fingers growing from our head.

Another crucial aspect of the health equation is RNA. If DNA is like the alphabet, RNA is the story written from it. Your lifestyle, environment, stress levels, and diet all influence how your genes are expressed. These factors can effectively 'turn on' or 'turn off' specific genes, directly shaping your health outcomes.

It's easy to blame genes for the onset of disease, yet less than 5% of diseases are directly caused by genetics. The majority of chronic conditions—such as type 2 diabetes, heart disease, and depression—are significantly influenced by lifestyle factors. This means we're not entirely bound by our genes; instead, we have the power to outsmart them by making intentional choices that promote and support our overall well-being.

Why do so many people believe their DNA is their destiny? It's rooted in outdated beliefs. When a grandparent died from a particular illness and a parent developed the same condition, it seemed inevitable that the next generation would face the same fate. However, it wasn't until the early 21st century that scientists discovered the truth.

In the late 1990s and early 2000s, scientists embarked on the ambitious Human Genome Project (HGP), a groundbreaking effort to map the entire human genetic code and gain a deeper understanding of DNA. In April 2003, the project reached a historic milestone by generating the first complete sequence of the human genome—a remarkable scientific achievement that offered crucial insights into the blueprint of humanity.

One of the key discoveries was that the human body contains approximately 23,000 protein-coding genes. In simpler terms, this means we have 23,000 biological blueprints, each containing instructions for producing the proteins essential for various functions in the body. Proteins serve as the building blocks for muscle growth, disease prevention, and metabolism regulation. This breakthrough led to a startling revelation that reshaped our understanding of genetics and health.

But the finding that humans have 23,000 genes initially confused scientists, because the number is surprisingly small. House plants have similar gene counts. So if our blueprints are no more complex than a houseplant's, how are we so sophisticated? The answer comes from understanding the tiny organisms that live within us.

If we look at the genes of the approximately 40 trillion microbes in and on our bodies, we see that theirs outnumber ours by about 100 to 1. Each microbe encodes 3,000–4,000 genes. Once we include our microbes in the total gene count, scientists learned that 99% of all the genetic material in our body doesn't come from our mom and dad. The bacterial genes that are referred to as the human microbiome have such an influence on physiological regulation that the medical community often recognizes them conceptually as an additional organ.

This is why, in recent years, there has been an explosion of microbiome-related health news and research. The activity of your microbes—whether they are working in harmony or out of balance—plays a significant role in determining whether you stay healthy or fall ill, as well as how quickly you age. Their activity directly influences which genes are activated, potentially leading to chronic disease or physical decline.

This made me wonder: what influences these microbes, RNA, and the activation of genes? The answer, I discovered, is *lifestyle*. How we move our bodies, manage stress, and, most importantly, what we eat all play a critical role in shaping these processes.

Myth 2: There's a one-size-fits-all healthy diet

For too long, we've treated our bodies like black boxes—putting in food without truly understanding what happens inside. Many of us assumed we were making the right choices by listening to experts, following doctors' advice, or adhering to generic food guides. However, this approach was often based on guesswork, because we lacked the tools to understand the unique chemical reactions in our bodies and determine which foods truly benefit or harm us.

That has changed. Viome has emerged as a pioneer in personalized nutrition, ushering in what we call Nutrition 2.0. We have built the largest gene expression database in the world, leading to groundbreaking health discoveries and debunking many common health and nutrition myths.

At the heart of this innovation is our AI-engine and software, Vie. It processes massive datasets far beyond human capacity, using machine learning and advanced mathematical techniques to decode the human healthscape. Vie has revealed that every individual's body is biochemically unique, and with each sample analyzed, it becomes more sophisticated. To date, Vie has processed over 1,000,000 samples, generating more than 100 quadrillion data points and enabling us to make meaningful connections faster and uncover insights that transform health outcomes.

As we've grown and collected more data, one of our major breakthroughs has been understanding that foods we commonly consider healthy may actually be harmful for some people. There is no universally healthy food or diet. For decades, we've been told to eat certain foods and avoid others, but data shows that what works for one person may not work for another. This concept is known as 'biochemical individuality.'

Even identical twins can respond to the same food in completely different ways. That's because every food is made of chemicals that interact with the chemicals in our bodies, and these interactions can lead to positive or negative health effects depending on the individual. To maintain vitality, it's essential to understand your body's unique data and use this information to calculate personalized dietary recommendations. Your biology holds the answers to what your body truly needs.

Eating, something we all do every day, should no longer be based on guesswork. With the right data, you can identify your superfoods and the foods that don't work for you.

Take spinach, for example. Long thought to be a superfood thanks to its iron, folate, and fiber, it's also one of the highest sources of oxalates.

Oxalates can bind to essential minerals like calcium, magnesium, and iron, preventing their absorption and affecting health. For some people, whose gut microbiomes cannot metabolize oxalates efficiently, spinach can increase the risk of issues like kidney stones.

Another example is grapefruit, often praised as a superfood for weight loss due to its low-calorie content and high water and fiber levels. However, grapefruit contains a compound that blocks the enzyme responsible for breaking down cortisol, the stress hormone. Elevated cortisol contributes to cravings and weight gain, meaning grapefruit can exacerbate these issues for people with already high cortisol levels.

Even turmeric, celebrated for its anti-inflammatory properties, can cause inflammation in certain cases. It stimulates the production of bile acids to help digest fats, but when the gut microbiome is unbalanced, these bile acids can be sent back to the liver, leading to inflammation and even fatty liver disease.

Before you label these foods as unhealthy, remember that your body's reaction to food is as unique as your fingerprint. Fad diets and one-size-fits-all eating plans promising universal benefits are misleading. True health comes from understanding what your body needs, which can now be determined through tools that analyze biological data from simple at-home tests.

Just like food, supplements should be customized to meet each individual's specific needs.

The key to thriving is knowing what your body needs and giving it the nutrients and foods to maintain balance and harmony. By doing this, you can begin to reverse aging and disease. Health is within your control, and staying vibrant as you age depends more on the choices you make each day than on accepting inevitable decline. Like a CEO overseeing key divisions of a company, you must monitor and manage the critical areas of your health to stay at your best.

Practice 3: Oversee and take action in the five areas

As health became a deep focus of mine, I noticed how much conflicting information exists in the health and wellness industries because of competing interests, personal bias, and money-making agendas. Knowing what to do to stay healthy can be difficult. So, to develop a better strategy, I began considering how to structure the vast scientific knowledge derived from years of research and data to make managing a person's health simpler.

As I considered these factors and how they are interrelated, I realized that we needed a framework to define them and keep them focused. I've also found there is a sequence to them, and that slightly new way to think about these five areas helps us consider what actions we need to take to stay healthy.

Thinking about how to organize the five critical areas of health brought me back to a theory that has been around for decades. You've likely heard of Maslow's Hierarchy of Needs. It's a framework developed by American psychologist Abraham Maslow that suggests humans are motivated by a tiered series of needs, starting with the most basic physiological necessities and ascending to the peak of self-actualization. He arranged these needs into five categories:

Maslow's Hierarchy of Needs

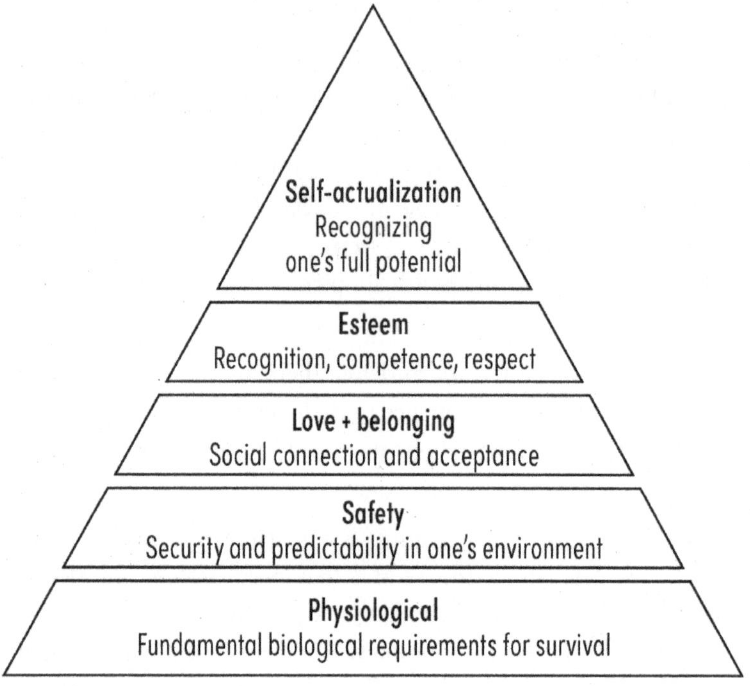

The hierarchy suggests that humans must satisfy lower-level needs before pursuing higher-level psychological and self-fulfillment desires, influencing behavior and personal growth. He asserted that if one need is unmet, a person cannot advance up the hierarchy to achieve the next need.

I realized that Maslow's lowest level—the physiological needs layer—has many sub-layers within it. To achieve physiological needs, we pretty much need another hierarchy altogether. To fulfill them, there is so much a person needs to know and do. We need to know what foods to eat, how to move and rest our body, and how to have healthy thoughts (because our brain is also part of our body).

There are five areas we know we need to focus on to stay healthy: nutrition, stress, fitness, sleep, and purpose. Managing these five is a job that's lifelong and requires daily focus. So, putting them into a model and breaking them down like Maslow did is one way to keep them in focus and ensure we are doing what we need to do to cover our health bases.

The Hierarchy of Longevity

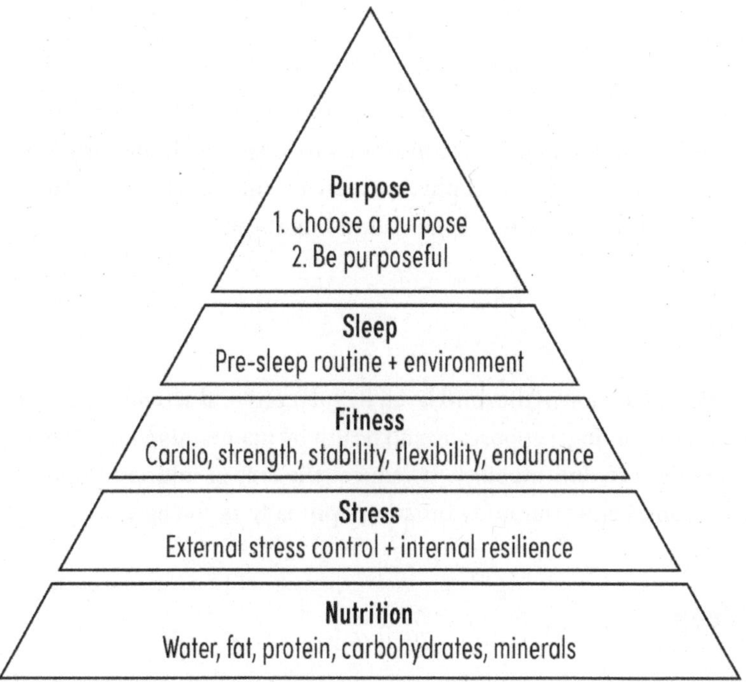

The Hierarchy of Longevity helps prioritize the actions we need to take in our life to optimize our health.

Let's examine each level and how they interconnect, working from the ground up.

Nutrition

Longevity begins with nutrition—it is the foundation of health. Just as a high-performance car needs the right fuel, your body requires nutrient-dense foods to operate at its best. Poor nutrition can cause deficiencies that disrupt progress in other areas of health, making it essential to tailor your diet to your unique and changing needs. Understanding precisely what your body needs is essential.

Stress

Stress management is the next layer of the hierarchy. Chronic stress disrupts bodily systems and contributes to long-term health problems. Practices like mindfulness, physical activity, and finding joy in simple pleasures can help restore balance and build resilience.

Fitness

Staying active forms the third layer. Regular physical activity, including strength training, supports overall health by maintaining muscle mass, bone density, and mobility. It reduces the risk of injuries, improves sleep, and helps your body function optimally as you age.

Sleep

Sleep is vital for recovery and rejuvenation. Quality sleep, with enough deep sleep and REM phases, supports physical repair, immune system health, and mental clarity. Prioritizing sleep ensures your body and mind can perform at their best.

Purpose

At the top of the hierarchy is purpose. Living with a sense of meaning and direction energizes and motivates you to make healthier choices, reduces stress, and fosters strong connections with others. Purpose is the ultimate driver of a fulfilling and healthy life.

Your health self-assessment

To thrive, start by assessing where you stand in each layer of the hierarchy and take actionable steps to improve your well-being. Make these areas a consistent focus, regularly reassess them, and set measurable milestones to track your progress. To do this effectively, stay informed about emerging science and apply it across all five areas. By doing this consistently, you can maintain and enhance your health. This might feel like taking on another job, and in many ways it is— but it's the most important job you'll ever have.

To succeed, combine the advice shared so far with additional steps to enhance your health journey. Surround yourself with the right people and supportive environments, create a vision or moonshot for your health, and apply the lessons from Chapter 4 to avoid common pitfalls—such as taking on too much, waiting for perfection, or living in denial of reality.

If you want to learn much more about my take on optimizing your health, read my book *The Youth Formula*. It examines precision medicine in a much deeper way and provides a framework on how to approach your health moving forward.

Prioritize your energy

After doing all this, you might still find there are times you get in the way of yourself when it comes to health. You might still deprioritize it. It is natural to have these moments, especially if you are living an extraordinary (and full) life. In the world we are in, it is easy to get off track at times.

This is another opportunity to be counterintuitive—to go against what most are doing. Most people will work those extra hours for more money even if their body needs sleep. But you can be someone who chooses to focus on your health first because you know you will function better. And that is easier, once again, if you measure your biometrics (the science) and use the right technology (the tools). It's harder to avoid the truth when it's in front of you.

Still, it will always be on you to make the choice to put health first, and that's an easier choice if you build your life around structures where health comes first. To make this work, you have to set clear rules for yourself. For instance, my morning hours are for learning, movement, and meditation. I have been in situations where I take too many calls to accommodate people in different time zones, but now I am much more particular about how I use these hours. If I don't protect this time, I'll sacrifice my health and destabilize everything else. Having external structures in place ensures I stick to these practices and remain the strongest, most present version of myself. Managing energy with intention is the foundation for achieving balance and success in all areas of life.

I want to finish our exploration of this topic with a final unconventional approach and story that might be what you need most when it comes to health. You might find that it changes everything.

In my journey with Viome, I have met many health experts. One that became a great friend and business partner is Dave Asprey, the father of biohacking. One day we were sharing strategies with a group we mentor, and Dave shared a nugget I could not agree more with, a framing of life and business that is so vital, I must pass it to you.

Dave explained that everything operates on energy mechanics, from the smallest part of your biology to the largest components of your business. It's all about energy balance. Without your conscious awareness, your body is constantly making trade-offs—deciding, for example, whether to prioritize making tissues to make you younger or stronger. This happens on every level: within cells, organs, networks, and even organizations.

Your business is the same way. Your life is too. If you want to optimize it, you have to optimize yourself. And, when it comes to the way you orient yourself around time, it is more effective to think from a perspective of managing energy.

If something drains your energy, delegate or outsource it. Many entrepreneurs, especially early in their careers, try to do everything themselves, which is counterproductive. So, be relentless about avoiding activities that deplete you. There's no need for judgment or justification for your preferences. Your likes and dislikes are emotional, not rational.

When you preserve and prioritize your energy, you can allocate it effectively to your mission, team, and creative pursuits. Managing your energy and putting your health first isn't selfish; it's strategic. Because as we all know, if you don't have your health, you have nothing.

Conventional thought trap

Many people deprioritize health for immediate goals because they feel fine, or because they are resigned to believing bad health and aging are inevitable, but the poor lifestyle choices that result inevitably catch up with them over time.

Counterintuitive approach

Health is the real wealth in life and should be prioritized. It gets easier when you think like a CEO and maintain your health as you would a business.

CHAPTER 8

COUNTERINTUITIVE PROBLEM-SOLVING

"Vision without action is merely a dream. Action without vision just passes the time. Vision with action can change the world."

—Joel A. Barker, futurist and author

IN 1995, I was working at Microsoft, one of the most powerful and influential companies in the world. Yet, I felt incomplete. I questioned whether I wanted to be an employee for the rest of my life or if, like the company's founder Bill Gates, I was meant to be an entrepreneur.

The internet was on the verge of transforming the world, and we were seeing the birth of companies like Netscape, Yahoo, Amazon, Lycos, Infoseek, and Excite. It was an era ripe for bold moves and innovative ideas. I realized that now was the time to start a groundbreaking company and that I needed to take bold actions of my own.

I had moments of doubt. Could I create my own company, or should I stay at Microsoft? I was no longer satisfied with working for someone else. I dreamed of running my own business. I wanted to see what I was truly capable of, even if it meant risking it all. Could I do it on my own? I had to find out.

So, one day I went into my boss's office and gave my notice. Just like that, I left my cushy Microsoft job. And then, I went home to tell my wife.

One giant leap

The house was unusually quiet, the rare kind of stillness that only occurred before my kids came back from school. My heart was pounding, not from what I had just done, but from what I was about to do.

I found Anu standing at the kitchen counter. She turned to look at me, her brow furrowing in confusion. "What are you doing home so early?" she asked.

I took a deep breath. "I quit," I said, letting the words hang in the air.

Anu's eyes widened. "You did *what*?"

I told her I had walked away from a nice salary, the millions in stock options, and the security of a job I excelled at—to chase an idea I didn't have yet. She stared at me, her eyes eventually narrowing. "Have you completely lost your mind?" she asked. "You don't even know what you're going to do next?"

The truth was, I didn't. I had no plan, no business model, and no clear timeline for how this wild leap would lead to a safe landing. All I had was a gut feeling—a belief that the internet was about to change everything and that I needed to be part of it. I told her we had enough money to survive for six months, maybe a year. It was enough for me to try.

Still, the weight of her doubt and visceral fear hit me hard. I couldn't let this decision drive a wedge between us. So, right then and there, I made a call. I dialed a friend I had made through Microsoft, put him on speakerphone, and asked a question I already knew the answer to: "If I need a job in six months, will you hire me?"

His response was immediate and almost amused. "Of course."

I hung up and turned to Anu. "Give me six months," I said. A hint of a smile tugged at her lips. And just like that, I had her reluctant approval.

Looking back, this might have been the first time I was truly thinking clearly. Ideas don't become reality on their own—you have to act on them. Taking action, even in the face of uncertainty, is what sets those who succeed apart from those who don't.

In the days that followed, doubts crept in, but that leap of faith was what led to my first major success: InfoSpace. It wasn't just a business; it became part of our family. Within a few years, it was worth over $40bn.

Even if InfoSpace had failed, I still would have succeeded because I took action to pursue a dream. I also would have grown and learned in ways my job at Microsoft could never have offered. Failure would have brought me closer to my next business success. This is the value of acting on our wildest ideas and dreams.

By jumping in and taking full responsibility, I discovered a sense of purpose and self-worth I had never felt before. For the first time, I wasn't working to realize someone else's vision. I was building something of my own. I had shifted my perspective in life and I now had a purpose. I was dreaming, acting on those dreams, and proving to myself that I could shape my reality and influence the world around me. It was a monumental time because I learned that pursuing dreams, even when they feel uncertain or irrational, is incredibly liberating. Every day as an entrepreneur, I felt more alive and empowered, knowing I was fully accountable for everything that happened, whether good or bad.

The experience taught me that success isn't defined by job titles or wealth; it's about having the courage to act, the resilience to persevere, and the satisfaction of bringing something new into the world. Even if you work within a company, you can be an *intra*preneur—taking initiative, driving results, and creating impact rather than waiting for instructions. That's what true success looks like.

You don't have to be perfect or wait for the ideal situation—what matters most is becoming a *doer*. The best entrepreneurs aren't the ones with the greatest ideas; they're the ones who execute. Without action, there are no results. There's also no substitute for the sense of control, purpose, and fulfillment that comes from creating and executing a vision. This is why those who take action ultimately win.

As I've learned over the years, it's the fear of taking action—especially being the first to do so—that holds most people back. Self-doubt often accompanies that initial leap. And even after you take action, staying the course on your mission can be incredibly challenging. Success isn't about a single action; it requires hundreds of them. You must remain steadfast, even when your situation feels hopeless.

Pursuing massive dreams will always present countless opportunities to stop and quit. The bigger question then becomes: how do you keep going?

The answer lies in having the right mindset—a counterintuitive one at that.

I won't spend much time on the basic day-to-day essentials—how to identify key metrics, or hire the right people. These foundational skills, often referred to as the 'blocking and tackling' of business, are relatively easy to learn.

One thing that isn't taught enough is the mindset needed to keep going when times get tough. To stay the course and reap the rewards, you need a specific kind of resilience—the mindset of someone who takes initiative and makes things happen rather than waiting for others to act.

The rewards of taking action

Before we dive into the mindset required to take action and stay the course to turn a vision into reality, I want to emphasize how simple it fundamentally is to make any big dream happen. Most people overcomplicate the process, which is why they spend more time thinking about taking action than actually doing it. Success in business and life becomes far less daunting when you break it down into components and approach it from a first-principles perspective.

First principles is a problem-solving framework used by scientists to tackle complex challenges by breaking them down into their most basic elements. A well-known example of this approach is Elon Musk's strategy for building SpaceX. Rather than accepting the high cost of purchasing pre-made rockets, Musk deconstructed the problem to its foundational components. He asked, "What are rockets made of?" and discovered that the raw materials—aluminum, titanium, copper—were far less expensive than buying a completed rocket. By focusing on these core components, Musk was able to build SpaceX rockets at a fraction of the traditional cost.

So, what if we take first principles and ask ourselves: What are the elements involved in achieving any extraordinary feat? The answer, you'll see, is fairly straightforward. To achieve a moonshot of any kind requires two elements, both of which are in your control. You must first:

1. Decide and commit to the outcome you want to achieve.

2. Take action to achieve it.

Once you know what you want, you start where you are. Then, you take the single smartest action that will move you closer to what you want. And then, from that one action, you get a result, which you learn from. After this, you repeat the process. You take the next smartest action.

To simplify this idea, the process of goal achievement is illustrated here:

The intuitive process of goal achievement

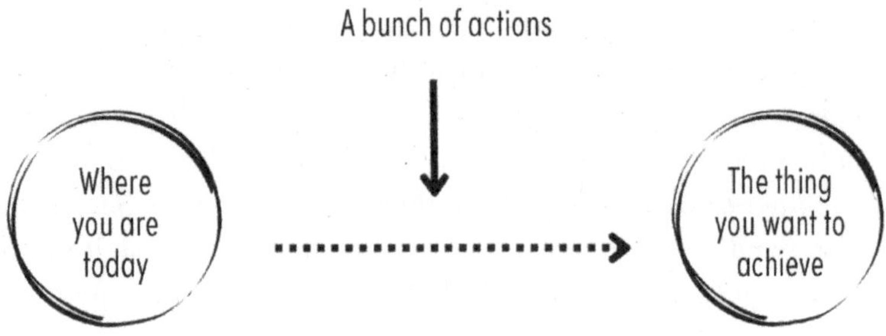

You should always have a macro-goal (or a few—one for each area of your life) alongside one or more micro-focuses. Missions should be big and inspiring, but execution starts small. Take a small, manageable slice of your mission and focus on it. Tackle one goal at a time. When you achieve one, the next will naturally emerge, and you can shift your focus to that.

The reality of the journey won't be this simple or straightforward, especially if you are aiming to realize a moonshot vision. It is much more likely to look like this:

The counterintuitive process of goal achievement

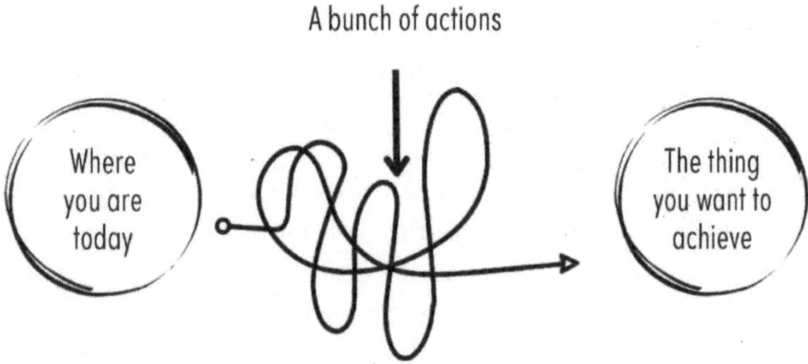

Although this path may seem like a squiggly mess of learning, pivots, and adapting plans, it ultimately boils down to a series of actions. The bottom line is simple: if you want something, take action—because ruminating about it on the couch won't get you far.

The greatest entrepreneurs and most successful people aren't those with the best ideas—they're the ones who take action. By doing, they achieve more, learn more, and continually improve at the skill of taking action. Action is what defines an entrepreneur. Without it, a person may be a visionary or a thinker, but not an entrepreneur.

Even if you don't run a business or aspire to, solving problems and taking action to create initiatives or bring dreams to life still makes you an entrepreneur in spirit. You're the kind of person who creates, participates in life, and drives results—and there's truly nothing like it.

On the other hand, if you spend too much time thinking and not doing, you can't fully participate in life. You'll find yourself stuck in imagined scenarios, endlessly thinking and dreaming but never making anything happen.

Most people have a deep, burning desire to create extraordinary things in this world. But people often struggle with change and can default to laziness or self-interest, driven by survival instincts and necessity. Adding to this challenge, we live in a world that doesn't always encourage people to pursue their dreams or take bold action.

Consider how most people are taught in their early years at school. They learn to follow instructions, wait for the teacher's guidance, and seek permission—raising their hand to speak. Bold ideas or attempts at collaboration are sometimes met with reprimands. It's easy to internalize these lessons and grow into a person who avoids risks, conditioned to fear failure and prioritize conformity over creativity.

Ask yourself: Do I want to make my dreams happen? Do I want to be someone who creates and brings new realities into existence, benefiting humanity? Do I want to live a life where I experience the dreams I envision?

I'm willing to bet your answer is yes. After all, you wouldn't be reading this book if you didn't want that.

You simply can't become that person if you don't take action. While this may seem obvious, before we dive into strategies for getting into action and staying the course—no matter how tough it gets—here are my top three reasons why you should stop thinking about that dream in your head and start taking action as quickly as possible.

Actions = results; no action = no results

Achieving any goal requires tangible action. To build the body you want, you need to exercise, eat well, and supplement appropriately. To create financial success, you must earn money through skills or effort, then manage it wisely in savings or investments to build wealth. Raising a capable adult starts with caring for their basic needs and evolves into teaching values, providing lessons, and fostering skills.

No outcome happens from mere thought; dreams only become reality through deliberate action. If you don't act, your dreams stay just that—dreams.

Outcomes create a feedback loop and a life of constant growth

Only by taking action can you get real-world feedback. The actions you take produce results that you learn from. Even if you fail or make mistakes, each action produces a result. Those outcomes give you important information about what works and what doesn't. Learning from each step refines your approach, increasing the chances of future success.

No matter what happens you are learning from experience, and there is no better way to learn. It is great to sit and study concepts, but you only truly get closer to the truth of a matter when you put that concept into practice.

Certainty from uncertainty, and the power of self-expression

Many people hesitate to take action because they perceive it as scary, uncertain, or risky. It's natural to fear that stepping into the unknown might threaten your sense of security. I felt this way when leaving my safe job at Microsoft. But what if I had stayed there for years, only to be let go, with limited experience outside that environment? Staying might have cost me the chance to build a life of greater certainty, control, and confidence—one where I shaped my own future and thrived on my own terms.

The supposedly scary, uncertain, and risky decision to step out on my own actually gave me far more security. I developed countless skills I wouldn't have gained at Microsoft. I became self-reliant and created a life where I had control over my financial destiny. More importantly, I built a life that feels authentic, self-expressed, and fulfilling.

Taking action consistently puts you ahead of those who only talk about their plans. If you examine any area where you've succeeded, it's because you took action. Even when opportunities seem to fall into your lap, they arise because of actions you took to create those possibilities. Conversely, any lack of results is tied to inaction.

So, what stops people? Why isn't the world full of action-takers and entrepreneurs? The answer lies in overcomplication. We tend to make the actions needed to achieve our goals seem far more daunting than they are. We struggle because of the emotions we attach to those actions—fear, doubt, and uncertainty. Often, it's not the actions themselves but the context we bring to them that holds us back.

That's why the rest of this chapter is dedicated to addressing the major mindset pitfalls and offering counterintuitive ways of thinking to help you avoid them. Consider this your toolkit—a mindset guide to help you persevere, take action, and stay the course.

Get in the arena and stay there

I once gave a lecture to a class of University of Washington students on entrepreneurship. During the talk, I shared a passage from President Theodore Roosevelt's famous speech at the Sorbonne in Paris. This quote is deeply personal to me—a transcript is framed on the wall of my office in Bellevue, Washington, a thoughtful gift from an employee. Even if you've heard it before, I encourage you to read it again and let it truly sink in:

> It is not the critic who counts; not the man who points out how the strong man stumbles or where the doer of deeds could have done better. The credit belongs to the man who is actually in the arena, whose face is marred by dust and sweat and blood; who strives valiantly; who errs and comes up short again and again, because there is no effort without error or shortcoming; but who knows the great enthusiasms, the great devotions, who spends himself for a worthy cause; who, at the best, knows in the end the triumph of high achievement, and who, at the worst, if he fails, at least fails while daring greatly, so that his place shall never be with those cold and timid souls who knew neither victory nor defeat.

Roosevelt's words are a powerful reminder of what it means to take action and embrace the struggle, rather than standing on the sidelines, paralyzed by fear of failure or criticism. It's not the observers or the critics who shape the world, but those who step into the arena, take risks, and face challenges head-on. Success and failure are secondary to the courage to pursue meaningful endeavors with passion and resilience. True fulfillment belongs to those who take action, knowing that even failure is honorable when it results from striving for something worthwhile.

The person in the arena is the one who gives 100% to life. This is the kind of person most people aspire to be. We all want to be the hero who fights and wins, the dreamer who makes their vision a reality. The problem isn't the desire to be in the arena—it's finding the courage to step in.

How do you enter the arena when the challenge ahead feels insurmountable? Especially when you've never been in such a space before? It's intimidating. Now imagine that the arena is filled with people watching your every move. How would that make you feel?

For many, the fear of what others think is enough to stop them. And even if you conquer that initial fear and step in, how do you *stay* in the arena when you're "marred by dust and sweat and blood," as Roosevelt says?

The answer is simple: you do it anyway. You commit, take the first small step, and keep moving forward. The more you act in spite of fear, the better you become at taking action. With every step, you build resilience, courage, and confidence.

With a lifetime of experience in business, I've observed that what stops most people isn't a lack of ideas or resources—it's their mindset and fear of failure. To stay in action, you often have to think counterintuitively and push against how you feel. You need to reframe your challenges and approach them with a mindset that keeps you empowered.

I've identified nine common pitfalls that prevent people from taking action, cause them to stop midway, or—tragically—hold them back even when they're on the brink of success. Let's explore these pitfalls and the strategies to overcome them, so you can step into the arena and stay there.

The nine most common mindset pitfalls that stop execution

When it comes to achieving what we want, the biggest roadblock in the way is ourselves. Here is my current list of the most common mindset pitfalls that take people out of the pursuit of their goal. There may be more, but these are the ones I see most often.

1. Waiting for perfect

2. Believing failure exists

3. Failing to trust intuition

4. Taking on too much too soon

5. Hiring clones of yourself

6. Letting cancer spread

7. Relating to stress as bad

8. Focusing too much on making money

9. Relying on conventional thinking

The rest of this chapter will get you to think differently about solving these problems. With a counterintuitive spin on any of them, you will see that they are caused by simple beliefs that *can* be changed. Once you challenge them, new thoughts give you access to a way forward. You become unstoppable.

Mindset pitfall 1: Waiting for perfect

Intuitive thinking: "It needs to be perfect."

Counterintuitive thinking: "Waiting only holds me back."

I'm not a sports person per se, but for a time, I owned a basketball team. Many evenings, I'd sit at center court, watching some of the greatest players of that era—Kobe Bryant and Michael Jordan.

I remember watching Kobe on nights when he'd take just five or six shots, each one landing perfectly, putting 12 or 15 points on the board. But then there were other nights when he'd take 50 shots, miss half of them, and still end up scoring 50 or 60 points. That, to me, is life. If you only take the shots you're sure will go in, you'll always be a 12-point player. If you want to be a 50-point player, you have to be willing to miss half of your shots and keep shooting.

The trick is accepting that half of what you do might not work—and that's okay. The moment you decide everything you do must succeed, waiting for it to be perfect or 'just right,' you'll only take safe shots. By doing that, you limit yourself and remain a 12-point player, never reaching your 50-point potential.

So, take shots—lots of them. Be in action. Life and business aren't about always making the 'right' decisions or waiting for perfect conditions. They're about making informed choices and learning through action. In many cases, you won't know what will work because you haven't tried it before.

It's also worth considering how dysfunctional it is to expect we should always know the perfect solution to a problem, especially when we lack experience. How egocentric is it to believe we can craft a plan or project that unfolds exactly as imagined? This isn't how reality works. In fact, the percentage of plans that go exactly as intended is shockingly low.

In the startup world, over 90% of companies pivot from their initial business plans due to unforeseen challenges, market shifts, or new insights. Similarly, in research and development, nearly 75% of initial approaches evolve as new discoveries are made. Overall, only a small proportion of plans in complex, dynamic environments unfold as originally expected.

It's better to launch your idea early and get real-world feedback instead of postponing your launch until you have a perfect product. You may completely miss the market window by waiting too long or, worse yet, miss out on users' feedback that would enable you to iterate and reiterate. I firmly believe that if you are not truly embarrassed by your initial version of the product launch then you have waited too long. I sometimes think back to the first few versions of the InfoSpace website and *I* feel embarrassed—but also proud that we launched early and used feedback to build the product that we have today. This is how most successful companies are built. Facebook was just a way to rate girls as 'hot or not' and it became the world's biggest social network as its developers learned more about what its users wanted.

Ultimately, what matters most is taking action and staying in action.

You can't wait around for the ideal moment. Success depends on adaptability and learning, not rigid adherence to a single plan. To achieve this, approach entrepreneurship—and anything else you do— as one big experiment. By viewing it this way, you allow room for discovery, growth, and the freedom to pivot as you learn.

Mindset pitfall 2: Believing failure exists

Intuitive thinking: "I might fail."

Counterintuitive thinking: "There is no failure, only learning."

Everything is an experiment. When you understand this, and choose to see business, your life, and the world this way, there is no such thing as failure. It simply doesn't exist. Every 'failure' is only a stepping stone closer to success. *Believing* in failure is the only way to actually fail.

Every time I start a company, the initial idea rarely matches what we end up creating. We start with a set of concepts and an overarching premise, but it always evolves significantly over time. For instance, when I launched Viome, our initial focus was on understanding the gut microbiome, which is responsible for expressing 90% of the genes in our bodies. We believed this was the key area to address. However, as we progressed, we realized that understanding the gut alone didn't provide a complete picture.

We discovered that interactions with the immune system and mitochondria were equally critical. This realization led us to expand our original Gut Health Test to include blood testing alongside stool testing, creating the Health Body Intelligence Test. At that point, we thought we had all the information we needed.

Then, we uncovered the significant role of the oral microbiome. Every day, we each swallow about one and a half liters of saliva, which directly impacts what happens in the gut. To truly complete the picture, we needed to analyze saliva, stool, and blood together. This breakthrough led to the development of Full Body Intelligence, a more comprehensive approach to understanding health.

We didn't have all the answers when we started. We began with a simple objective: to understand what changes in the human body when people get sick. And everything we did was one big experiment towards that goal. Our moonshot never changed, but our approach evolved constantly as we learned. In fact, we never set out to build at-home test kits. We had no idea what to expect, nor did we fully appreciate what we'd need to do to gain that understanding.

Similarly, when I left Microsoft to launch my first business, I approached it as an experiment. I started with a simple premise: Build an internet business that solves a massive problem most people are facing. My second big goal was to create a business that provided something essential—a service or product everyone needed but didn't yet realize they needed.

Coming from outside the industry, I had a perspective that differed from most. While everyone in technology was focused on building recognizable brands like Yahoo, I saw an opportunity from a different angle. In every major industry, the biggest successes often came from those who provided the essential tools.

During a gold rush, it isn't only the luckiest prospectors who get rich—it is also the people selling shovels and picks. So, I thought, why not provide the shovels and picks for everyone building their brand on the internet? I envisioned a company that would provide essential content as a private-label service. If someone built a website, they'd need content—and we could be their Reuters for whatever information they required.

And so, I went to work, trying to figure out what that essential information was by researching common needs and activities that could be done more efficiently over the internet. I soon realized I might be able to help people find phone numbers as a place to start.

Like most businesses, the beginning was clunky and manual and not glamorous. This is how you work to prove concepts and then you evolve from there.

As we evolved, we went from offering phone numbers to business listings, stock quotes, even horoscopes, often branded under the names of our client companies. We became the content provider behind the scenes, letting them take the credit. Eventually, we took out a full-page ad in *The Wall Street Journal* showcasing all the brands that used our services. In small print, behind each brand, was 'InfoSpace.' The message was clear: You may not know us, but you use us every day.

When you start with a massive premise and approach it as an experiment, you'll realize there's rarely a definitive moment where you choose to abandon the idea entirely. However, there are times when it's necessary to pivot or let go of a business idea that isn't producing the desired results. Almost every successful company has faced near-death moments. SpaceX, Facebook, and Twitter, for example, all encountered significant challenges that required them to pivot to survive and thrive.

For struggling companies, there will come a time when pivoting is a better choice than giving up. If the path you've chosen isn't working, choose a different one. The key is to keep the core purpose of your company alive. You may need to give up on the initial execution plan, but never on the purpose behind it.

Before starting a company, prepare yourself with multiple plans—Plan A, B, C, D, E—and when those fail, you need plans X, Y, Z, and beyond. The idea is to stay flexible and committed to your purpose. Remember: your purpose doesn't die, and you don't give up until you reach your destination.

An experiment also doesn't have to succeed for you to progress. Instead, it provides information on what to do next. People often say, "What happens if I fail?" but when you're experimenting there's no such thing as success or failure—only different outcomes. If outcome A happens, what are the parameters you'll change in your next experiments? Likewise with outcome B? You approach each goal as a new experiment, with no need to label it as a success or failure. The only real failure is giving up. This is as true with business dreams as it is with personal ones. Everything else is just another experiment on the path to finding the solution you're looking for.

The best way to approach business and life is to adopt a mindset like Thomas Edison's. Start with a premise—a problem you want to solve or an area you want to explore—then take action, learn, and iterate. Edison famously set out to create the light bulb and is often said to have failed 1,000 times. However, he didn't view his attempts as failures; for him, each one was part of the experiment. This relentless experimentation and learning process is what ultimately led to his success.

The more experiments you do, the more you learn. Try to 'fail fast.' It's about how quickly you can test an idea, observe the outcomes, and adapt. Each experiment provides insights that guide your next steps, making each attempt a stepping stone toward greater success.

Mindset pitfall 3: Failing to trust intuition

Intuitive thinking: "I focus on spreadsheets and data."

Counterintuitive thinking: "Intuition is its own form of decision-making data."

There's a lot of uncertainty and a lack of available information when you're taking a path less traveled. You have to rely on clues and intuition to make decisions, not spreadsheets.

Spreadsheets can mislead you. When you believe in a certain outcome, confirmation bias can lead you to make optimistic assumptions about unknown variables. Conversely, when you don't have faith in an outcome, you tend to make pessimistic assumptions. Often a spreadsheet will only tell you what you are already thinking.

I use a different approach. If I have to make an important decision early in a venture, I close my eyes and visualize having made the decision. I simulate how I would feel about it now and imagine the impact three-to-five years into the future. This process allows me to rely on my intuition and mentally simulate outcomes, free from the emotional bias of numbers.

Spreadsheet numbers may be precise, but they're often based on incorrect assumptions. Yet we tend to treat them as unassailable unless we step back to challenge those assumptions.

I hired a Harvard MBA at Intelius, my information commerce company. In his first month, we came across a company I believed would be a good acquisition to serve as a foundation for launching a new business. I asked him to follow up and come back with his recommendations. He spent weeks building a sophisticated model and concluded that it didn't make sense to acquire the company at the price they would demand.

I didn't even look at his model. Instead, I asked him to describe his conclusions and reasoning. But he kept referring back to his model's calculated valuation. Finally, I told him, "This new business opportunity is ripe, based on where the market is headed. Acquiring this company will give us a solid foundation to launch and capture market share."

As you might guess, he had assumed all the unknowns with pessimistic projections. His spreadsheet simply reinforced what he already believed. I used my intuition to make the decision to acquire the company. That led to a new business that ultimately became worth twice as much as Intelius.

You have to trust your gut instincts, believe in yourself, and have confidence that you can win the games you're playing. Many people think entrepreneurs are big risk-takers. I say the best ones are risk-averse. They play games they know they can win because they have the right intuition.

Mindset pitfall 4: Taking on too much too soon

Intuitive thinking: "I always need to do one more thing."

Counterintuitive thinking: "I avoid indigestion."

One of the main reasons businesses fail is a lack of focus. Most companies don't die from starvation—they die from indigestion. In other words, they fail not because they're doing too few things, but because they're trying to do too many things.

Focus is absolutely key to entrepreneurial success. It's easy to fall into the trap of thinking, *wow, look at that company—they're making so much money! I should do what they're doing.* Or, you think you're succeeding with one product and should focus on another before the first is solidly a success. But the reality is, chasing every opportunity only spreads you thin and derails your progress.

To maintain focus, I follow a principle I call the Rule of Three. Counterintuitively, the Rule of Three is really about doing *one* thing at a time. Here's how it works:

1. **The primary focus:** This is the one thing I spend 80% of my time on. It's the core of the business, the main driver of success, and the area where I focus most of my energy. This singular focus is critical because it ensures the company's foundation is solid and growing. You have to be fully committed to a single goal—the hill you're willing to die on. If it doesn't work after trying absolutely everything, then you need the discipline to pivot and move on to the next thing. But you cannot pursue two major goals simultaneously. Splitting your focus will only ensure that neither succeeds.

2. **The next big thing:** While I'm focused on the primary task, I spend about 15% of my time nurturing something that has the potential to be the next big opportunity. These are small 'skunk works' projects—experimental initiatives designed to test if an idea could become the next big thing. I allocate a small amount of time and resources to these projects to see if they can succeed. I don't let it distract me from the primary focus, but I invest just enough time to develop and evaluate its potential. If the primary focus matures or begins to plateau, this 'next thing' is ready to step in. By the time the main business is maturing and growing incrementally, I have already built the next growth engine.

3. **Exploring the unknown:** The remaining 5% of my time is spent learning about completely new areas—emerging trends, innovations, or threats that could impact the company. This is about staying curious, identifying potential disruptions, and preparing for the future. I use this time learning about things I know nothing about in emerging fields I'm unfamiliar with. I want to constantly expand my understanding. For example, I want to learn everything I can about generative models—what they can and cannot do. I may not know how to apply them yet, but I want to be prepared because if these technologies start to make an impact, I need to understand how they could transform my business. This is where new moonshots come from. An idea that may take three-to-five years to mature while you are still experimenting.

This framework allows me to stay laser-focused on what matters most today while keeping an eye on the future. It also prevents the temptation to chase every shiny new opportunity, which often leads to burnout and failure. Focus is the foundation of success, and the Rule of Three ensures that I'm always building for today, tomorrow, and beyond.

Mindset pitfall 5: Hiring clones of yourself

Intuitive thinking: "I like to work with friends."

Counterintuitive thinking: "I hire those with skills I *don't* have."

The first challenge you face when starting a company is building a team. It's one of the most critical and difficult aspects of launching a business: How do you build the right team around you?

When you're looking for a friend, you tend to seek out someone who is just like you—someone who shares your interests, enjoys the same activities, and resonates with you on the same emotional wavelength. If you like concerts, they like concerts. If you enjoy going out for drinks, they do too. You gravitate toward people who are almost a mirror image of yourself, and it works well for friendships because you connect and enjoy each other's company. But that's *not* how companies are built.

Companies succeed when you surround yourself with people who *complement* you, not replicate you. These individuals bring completely different skills, perspectives, and strengths to the table. For instance, if you're a visionary—someone who sees the big picture and sets the direction—they might not fully understand your vision, and that's okay. They're the ones who are excellent at building the roads while you focus on cutting through the trees.

Building a successful company is like assembling the pieces of a puzzle. Each piece has a unique role to play, and together, they create the full picture. Think of it as a living organism: a body needs a variety of organs, each with its distinct function. The heart can't act like the lungs, and the kidneys can't replace the brain. Every organ is different, yet they all work together to keep the body alive and thriving.

Don't hire people just because you'd enjoy hanging out with them. Instead, hire people who can perform the roles you can't—who can be the organs your company needs. A body with ten hearts wouldn't survive without lungs, kidneys, and so on. The same principle applies to a company. Diversity in skills, perspectives, and functions is what makes it work.

When building your team, you should also be careful not to hire someone solely for their skills. This is because you can teach skills, but you can't teach attitude. A new hire's work ethic and commitment is more important than their current skill set. The exception is if those skills are a requirement for your business and highly specialized. For instance, my chief technology officer and chief medical officer were key to Viome's success because our products depend on highly specialized AI knowledge and systems biology. However, other than highly specialized skills the product creation depends on, many skills can be learned.

When you find someone with a great attitude and a genuine desire to learn, you can teach them the necessary skills, and they will grow with the company. One of the most impactful things I've done is to prioritize hiring smart, passionate individuals who care deeply about our mission and truly believe in what we're working to achieve. These are the people who can learn, adapt, and grow alongside the company, becoming invaluable over time.

Committed people with different working styles, backgrounds, and skills come together to form a team of superheroes with different superpowers who share that deep commitment to the mission. There is nothing more powerful.

Mindset pitfall 6: Letting cancer spread

Intuitive thinking: "I'll deal with this problem later."

Counterintuitive thinking: "I do not let cancer spread."

You are bound to make hiring mistakes. Even with incredible mission-driven experts there will be conflict and ego clashes that you don't anticipate. Building anything with people also means human error is a factor. People make mistakes— sometimes big ones that impact the team, business, and mission.

The key is to correct those mistakes immediately. When it's a human error problem, take it on as yours without blame. Do your best to take the morality out of the situation. For instance, let's say a teammate takes on too many projects and becomes overwhelmed. This leads to a product that launches with an incorrect label. Instead of blaming the person, get to the bottom of how it happened by seeing it through the lens of actions and outcomes. How did an action or series of actions lead to the outcome? Then, create a new structure so it won't happen again. For a situation like this, you might create a rule that no one in the company has more than two projects at once. Or you can make sure that your team all abide by the Rule of Three.

Just as it's crucial to hire fast, it's equally important to fire fast when you recognize that one of your hires is a bad fit. Every time I delayed addressing a bad hire, it cost me significantly—and sometimes nearly destroyed the company. When you intuitively know someone isn't the right fit—whether they don't align with the company's culture or aren't collaborating effectively—it's critical to act. Even if they are highly skilled at their job, if they aren't contributing to the overall organism of the team, they become a detriment. Imagine a cell in the body that stops cooperating with others and begins functioning independently. That's cancer. A cancerous cell grows unchecked, disrupts the harmony, and starts corrupting the organism. If it's not addressed and removed, it spreads, and the entire body suffers as a result.

The same concept applies to a culture. A team member who prioritizes their own agenda over the collective good can poison the culture. Their selfish behavior can spread, influencing others and creating a toxic environment. When that happens, the company begins to suffer irreparably. That's why, as soon as you identify this type of cancer, you need to take immediate action to remove it. Doing so not only protects the organization but also sends a clear message: the team's immune system will not tolerate toxicity or misalignment.

Firing people is not fun. No one ever thinks, *who can I fire today to cheer me up?* It's a serious decision, and it never brings joy. Even if you get used to doing it over time, it's not something you wake up excited to do. It should never be about power or ego. It should always be about the mission, the purpose, and the greater good of the company. The decision to let someone go should come only when their presence begins to compromise the purpose your company set out to achieve.

The key point is that the responsibility lies with you. When a hire doesn't work out, it's not the person's fault—it's yours. You made the decision to hire them, believing they were the right fit. When that turns out to be wrong, it's a time for introspection, not blame. Instead of taking joy in the act, you reflect on where you went wrong. What red flags did you miss? What questions could you have asked during the interview process that might have revealed more? The experience becomes a learning opportunity to improve your hiring process for the future.

Mindset pitfall 7: Relating to stress as bad

Intuitive thinking: "I can't wait to have a smooth life."

Counterintuitive thinking: "Ups and downs mean I'm alive."

Ups and downs are a natural part of life. It's not the case that 'ups' are good and 'downs' are bad. To become great at managing them, first accept this reality and then work with it. Avoiding or fighting the stress of ups and downs (which is what most people do) will not help you succeed at anything. Learn to ride the roller coaster.

Getting good at managing stress is first about recognizing that it *can* be innately good. The Yerkes-Dodson Law proposes that there is an optimal level of stress that can boost focus, motivation, and productivity. Too little stress, on the other hand, can lead to underperformance because of overwhelm and lack of motivation. The Yerkes-Dodson Law highlights that a balanced level of stress is essential for achieving peak performance.

Does that mean you should now go take on super stressful things? No, be smart about it. Generally, people suck at dealing with stress because few are taught how to deal with it well. You can't control the world, but you can certainly control how you react to it. Our outlook and beliefs around actions and results create stress. This piece of advice is about reframing the actions you take—as well as their results—so that you no longer view them as 'good' or 'bad.'

Every action you take produces an outcome, and *the meaning you ascribe to it* dictates whether you believe it is good or bad. Meaning simply comes from perspective and context, which in turn come from what you believe and have learned up until that point in your life. This is why (as we first learned in Chapter 2) we often find that, with time, something we once thought was negative actually turns out to be beneficial.

The simplest way to understand this is for us to go back to the story I told you in Chapter 4 about my first encounter with snow and extreme cold. Allowing it to upset me just made the effect of the cold worse. Then one day, taking a counterintuitive view, I saw the snow as something good, and I felt good too. Yet, it was still the same white flakes falling from the sky. What changed was my perspective. My filter—the labels of 'good' or 'bad'—shaped my experience of the snow and of life. Everything can shift in an instant if we're willing to recognize that, in reality, good and bad are simply constructs of our minds.

If everything is always smooth sailing, you're probably not challenging yourself enough. Growth happens when you push boundaries, and that often brings discomfort. It introduces stress, but the kind of stress that fuels progress, not harm.

Everyone faces tough times, and in those moments, it's essential to stay grounded and believe in yourself. Trust that the next upbeat is coming. However, when you're at the peak, remember to stay humble. Challenges will return—winter always comes. It's a cycle, and humility will carry you through both the highs and lows.

When I encounter these moments, I rely on principles and phrases that guide me through stress. They remind me that this is all part of a greater journey. There's no absolute good or bad—there's only what is.

When you have that attitude, you keep pushing forward through every hurdle that comes your way. The beauty of life is enjoying everything that happens.

Mindset pitfall 8: Focusing too much on making money

Intuitive thinking: "I need to make more money."

Counterintuitive thinking: "I need to improve more lives."

I often get asked on podcasts and in interviews: How do you build a billion-dollar business? I always say that to make money you should not be overly focused on dollars and cents. If you are, you will find you can only get to a certain level before hitting a ceiling. You might make some money but you will feel unfulfilled no matter where you get it.

We've covered this before so I will only touch on it again briefly here, but I see this all the time with entrepreneurs, so I want to expand a little.

As entrepreneurs, we want money because it is about survival, freedom, self-expression, and impact. But often we earn the money only to realize that we only achieved survival and not the freedom, self-expression, or impact aspects we truly want. Making money is a byproduct of improving lives. If you focus on that, you will succeed.

Now, there is a nuance here to understand: you can focus on improving lives all day and you can make a living and feel good about yourself and your contribution to the world. But to be very successful in business you have to do it *at scale*. Then you will also have more money to invest in doing it again.

Money alone can't motivate you to take great risks and endure the difficulties of entrepreneurship, because there are so many other jobs out there which are more likely to make you rich. Only great enthusiasm, great devotion, and a worthy cause can make a successful entrepreneur, because truly believing in what you are doing is the only way to make it through the sacrifices and challenges that will beset you.

Mindset pitfall 9: Relying on conventional thinking

Intuitive thinking: "We need an expert."

Counterintuitive thinking: "We need a different perspective."

Malcolm Gladwell talks about needing 10,000 hours to gain world-class expertise in your field. I've always found that idea puzzling. I believe that once you become an expert, you often become an incrementalist.

What do I mean by that? The best of the best can be 10% better than others, but you can never be ten times better by following the same rules. To achieve that level of improvement, you have to challenge the very foundations that experts take for granted. You have to think differently about the problem—and that kind of thinking usually comes from someone who is new to the industry.

It's not just about thinking *outside the box*; it's about thinking in a completely different box. In other words, it's applying knowledge from one industry to solve problems in another. It's about connecting dots that have never been connected before.

Take the Wendy Schmidt Oil Cleanup XCHALLENGE as an example. This was a competition to find innovative solutions for cleaning up oil spills. For 50 years, the industry had relied on the same outdated technology. The XPRIZE Foundation wanted to see if someone could drastically improve the process. Here's the surprising part: not a single team in the finals came from the oil spill cleanup industry. One of the finalist teams consisted of a mechanic, a dentist, and an artist from a tattoo parlor.

This team approached the problem with a completely fresh perspective. Their concept was inspired by water skiing, and worked a bit like a vacuum cleaner pulling a massive storage bag across the water to collect oil. This unconventional solution turned out to be four times faster than the industry standard.

True breakthroughs often come from outsiders who aren't limited by conventional thinking. To achieve outsized results, you have to question everything the experts assume. You have to be willing to explore a different box altogether.

Whenever you feel stuck on your journey toward achieving a goal, get curious. Ask different questions. The sooner you turn a challenge into a problem to be solved—by thinking about it from a new perspective—the better positioned you'll be to stay in action and keep improving.

This is what it means to persevere, to cultivate the skill we call 'grit,' and to stay the course. Ultimately, it's all about your mindset. The way you think determines whether you keep going or give up.

Mindset isn't everything

If you follow this guidance and work on your mindset, making adjustments along the way, you'll find your approach to building a business or reaching any goal becomes much easier. It's incredible how getting into the right headspace can make tackling a moonshot far more achievable.

That said, mindset alone isn't everything. You, and you alone, well, that won't get you far either. You need to build relationships and be smart about it too. We'll focus on that next.

Conventional thought trap

Most people get stuck in 'analysis paralysis,' overthinking and waiting for the perfect moment to act—but that moment rarely comes, and inaction often leads to missed opportunities and unfulfilled potential.

Counterintuitive approach

Success comes from taking action, not just dreaming or planning, because ideas only gain value through execution, and each step forward provides feedback, knowledge, and unexpected opportunities. *Do* more than you *think* about doing and you will succeed.

CHAPTER 9

COUNTERINTUITIVE RELATIONSHIPS

"Don't sell yourself short; you are your best asset."

—Matshona Dhliwayo

I N 2024, I had a deep desire to help entrepreneurs expand their businesses and think on a larger scale. And so, I launched a mentorship program called Apollo Group.

One of the most beautiful aspects of this group is how the members became like family. We'd get together virtually and in-person. We'd travel and attend conferences and events together. Members even stayed in one another's homes when they were in the same city. Because of this close-knit bond, we were very selective about who we brought into the group. We prioritized individuals who shared our values. Our goal was to build authentic relationships with like-minded people who think big and to nurture a mindset where every member of the group was constantly growing.

At a conference in which the Apollo Group was featured, our group director brought a potential member by the VIP lounge to meet everyone and gauge whether he would be a good addition to the family.

When we asked the prospective member—let's call him Mike—about his interest in joining us, he launched into a canned pitch to prove how awesome he was by telling us about all the impressive people he knew. Finally, I interrupted him. "In the last five minutes, all we've learned about you is that you know everyone from Deepak Chopra to Tony Robbins. But we know nothing about *you*. Who are you and what drives you?"

I told him no one in our group had a big ego. What we were looking for was people with a clear mission and purpose, who are authentically interested in bringing great businesses to the world and building deep relationships. I challenged him to re-share who he was from the perspective of the value he would bring to the group beyond his personal connections. I asked him what makes him want to get up in the morning.

Mike stopped talking and looked at me like a little boy who just got caught by the teacher for sneaking a peek at a schoolmate's math test. He then spent the next five minutes telling us about his business struggles and his 'why' in the world, which seemed very inauthentic.

We decided to take a pass on Mike. I later learned he had made a showy first impression on our group director the day prior. He came to talk to her with an entourage of assistants and an air of self-importance (another clue that he was not right for the group).

So many people feel the need to lead with their accomplishments and connections to prove their worth. They need to brag or display how great they are in some way. But people respect other people who are genuine, people who own their strengths and weaknesses and know what they stand for in life.

Truly successful people, those who do meaningful work in the world, don't flaunt their status. They don't need to because their actions and accolades are a demonstration of their work and worth in the world. When a person is making a massive effort to prove their worth, it signals that they don't truly believe they are worthy or that they are hiding something—usually that they haven't done what they say they have.

Attempting to show up as perfect, exceptional or better than everyone else is a waste of time. People value sincerity and, when it is present, it makes them want to connect. No one wants to build relationships with people they feel are hiding something. I've learned that the more you can be yourself—the good, the bad, all of it—the more respect you earn.

When you embrace and understand who you are, along with the values you live by and stand for, you naturally attract genuine, like-minded individuals who bring positivity and great opportunities into your life. On the other hand, the more you feel the need to prove yourself, the more you attract others who are similarly driven by ego. Building meaningful relationships that open doors and make life fulfilling starts with being authentically *you*.

This is where counterintuitive thinking can help. It requires asking for help when you don't know the answer, being upfront about your imperfections, owning what you think is flawed about yourself or your approach. And what's funny about this is that you will find that when you do this you will be seen as more of a 'perfect' person! Confident people don't know everyone and everything. They understand what they do and don't know, and they are honest and upfront about it. This is how they show up with the kind of authenticity that attracts great people and opportunities to them.

Humility is a true sign of success. If you are still arrogant then you are still trying to prove something to yourself or others. The day you become humble is the day you become successful, because you no longer feel the need to prove anything to anyone, including yourself.

Be genuine and people will experience you as confident, trustworthy, and likeable

Growing up with limited resources may have made me less egotistical than most at a young age. I had nothing to prove, because, quite literally, *I had nothing* to prove! Being genuine came naturally to me, and it worked in my favor. Early on, I learned an invaluable lesson: if I was unapologetically myself, that was all I needed to be to go far in life.

This lesson has been reinforced countless times and has led to many successes in both my life and career. In fact, it played a pivotal role in my journey—it's how I earned a computer engineering scholarship to come to America, despite having no prior knowledge of computers. Let me share this wild story with you. Not only will it prove my point, but it might also inspire you to consider how you show up in the world and why being genuine is one of the most attractive and powerful traits for so many reasons.

While I was in college, a corporate recruiting fair was held on campus. As part of the event, students had the opportunity to take a technology aptitude test administered by select companies offering contract positions with computer programming firms in the United States. Since I wasn't pursuing computer engineering at the time, I didn't sign up for the tests. Instead, I spent the day enjoying the beautiful weather, working on class assignments.

To get from the halls where the tests were being administered back to the dormitories, students had to walk along a central boulevard. I happened to be sitting and reading on some steps under the clear, blue sky. Groups of students passed, chattering excitedly and debriefing each other in rapid-fire exchanges. At first, I paid little attention, though the thrill in their voices was unmistakable. Gradually, as more students gathered nearby, I began catching snippets of their conversation. "That was impossible," one said. "I wasn't sure about any of those questions," another added.

Curious, I started asking questions: What were they tested on? What were the subjects? What was each section about? How much tech jargon did they need to know? At first, they laughed. Then one of them asked, "You're serious, aren't you?"

I told them I was, which made them laugh even more. Still, they explained the structure of the tests. Since they had taken two different exams, they couldn't give me exact answers but helped me understand the format. The more I listened, the more it sounded like a general aptitude test rather than a deep technical assessment. I asked if there was still time to take it, and they mentioned another session later in the day, though they weren't sure if it was full.

As I got up to leave, they joked they'd wait for ten minutes, just in case I came back defeated. I signed up for the next session and when the results came in, I'd done well enough to attract the attention of several recruiters eager to meet me.

During the formal interview with the company representatives from U.S. business equipment maker Burroughs, I felt a bit shakier than during the test. They mostly asked general questions, and I quickly realized they knew I wasn't a programmer. Looking back, I wasn't fooling anyone with my limited computer knowledge, but given my test score, I wondered if they were seeking people they could train.

One man, thin with thick glasses and a shirt soaked from the humidity, interrupted his partner's questioning to get to the point. "Do you know the difference between a bit and a byte?" he asked, with a smug look, clearly hoping to disqualify me.

But I didn't panic. I had come into this with nothing to lose. At worst, I'd learn that I wasn't suited for computer engineering. After a moment of thought, I looked him in the eyes, smiled, and put my thumb and forefinger close together. "Bit, small," I said. Then, spreading my fingers as wide as I could, I added, "Byte, big." I knew that much.

A few days later, I was offered a contract position with Burroughs in the United States. Through this experience, I learned that embracing your flaws and showcasing them authentically can resonate deeply with others. When you acknowledge your mistakes or quirks, you build trust and foster genuine connections.

People connect with humble, honest individuals—not with those who seek to project perfection. This is because authentic people can be trusted and respected, which are the two elements of all great relationships. So, it pays to 'just' be you: others will trust and respect you for it.

The two foundational ingredients of great relationships

Most people believe success depends on 'who you know,' but that's not true. Who you know simply opens the door for you. The people in your network must also *like* you before they will help you. And for a person to like you there are two elements they need to experience when they interact with you.

Those two elements are:

1. Trust

2. Respect

Defining and measuring these qualities can be difficult, because they are inherently subjective. However, trust remains the cornerstone of any relationship, whether personal or professional. Before people consider your capability to handle a task, they first evaluate whether they can trust you. Trust is often experienced as a sense of warmth—a 'vibe,' for lack of a better word, that signals your good intentions and genuine care for others.

Respect, on the other hand, is earned when you demonstrate that you are competent. People respect others when they bring value to situations because they add to or elevate them. Once trust is established, competence reinforces it. It's showing that you can deliver on your intentions and follow through on commitments.

Think of it this way: when you hire a nanny, you're choosing someone you trust to care for your most precious asset—your children. However, trust alone doesn't mean you plan to invest in their next entrepreneurial venture. For deeper relationships or investment, respect is equally important. This is especially true in business. When people respect you for your conduct, intellect, or vision, they're far more likely to invest in you and your ideas.

Trust is built on a foundation of honesty and unwavering integrity. A reputation for honesty is crafted over time, brick by brick, through consistent actions that reflect these values. Honesty is not a commodity you can buy or a task you can delegate—it must be earned through genuine effort. In today's hyperconnected world, where information travels at the speed of light, a hard-earned reputation can be lost in an instant. Honesty and integrity leave no room for compromise; you're either all in or you're all out. As my friend Sir Richard Branson wisely puts it, "All you have in business is your reputation."

So, it's very important that you keep your word by honoring what you say you will do. Once you build a respected reputation, it also serves as the best advertisement for your business. No marketing tool is as powerful as a positive reputation. Even without advertising, your business can grow through word of mouth. Your integrity is the most effective marketing mechanism in the world. When people know they can trust you and recognize your good reputation, they are far more likely to do business with you and recommend you to others. Being someone who wants the best for others leads to higher customer satisfaction, increased brand loyalty, and a stronger standing in the marketplace. Moreover, a well-earned reputation can also shield your company from legal or regulatory challenges, which can be both costly and damaging.

A single act of dishonesty can destroy years of hard work and damage your career. Therefore, when faced with difficult decisions, it's crucial to consider not only the short-term gains but also the long-term consequences. Many people fail to recognize this, but behaving ethically and honestly is always the best long-term choice, both morally and economically. While making ethical decisions may not always be easy or immediately profitable, it is ultimately the right path to take for both personal and professional success.

You, and you alone, get to define what you stand for, regardless of the business you're in. Because no two people have the same sense of ethical behavior or hold identical value systems, it is up to you to draw any and all ethical lines. In business, and in life, there are few times someone will ask you, "are you comfortable with this?" but many times you should refuse to go along.

In business, there are countless factors beyond your control: how consumers will perceive a product, the effectiveness of an advertisement, how you're treated in the workplace, or the state of the economy. What you can control is how you conduct yourself and respond to the challenges that arise. Your level of professionalism is entirely within your power.

Next, let's explore how to cultivate these qualities and the remarkable benefits of being a good-natured, competent individual—someone others trust and respect. There are four essential principles we need to understand here:

1. Attracting teammates, investors, and customers is about sharing your truth.

2. Focus on relationships to unlock abundance in all areas.

3. Build lasting relationships, not transactions, and know the difference.

4. To be unstoppable, fall in love with yourself.

Now let's unpack each one.

Principle 1: Attracting teammates, investors, and customers is about sharing your truth

Sharing your truth is a very powerful tool. When you are clear on who you are, what you stand for, and your moonshot, all you need to do is share it with passion.

I use the word 'sharing' intentionally, rather than 'communicating' or 'telling,' because sharing better captures the essence of the action. When you share, you're offering a gift of information to others. If you're confident, grounded, and articulate, and if you convey your message effectively, it will resonate. People won't just hear your words; they'll be moved by them—and that's exactly what you want to achieve.

To make this happen, I've developed a process for it. If you've already done the work outlined earlier in this book to clarify your moonshot, this will come naturally.

Most entrepreneurs focus on explaining what they do, assuming that's what investors care about. But entrepreneurs must understand that investors are just as interested in *them* as they are in their moonshot. Who is the person they're backing? What drives them? Are they simply motivated by making money, or do they have a genuine purpose? Every investor knows that entrepreneurs will inevitably face tough times. Those driven solely by quick money often walk away when challenges arise. On the other hand, entrepreneurs with a deep sense of purpose push through the walls and endure the downs long enough to see the ups.

While investors care about the vision—what the world will look like if you succeed—they are ultimately investing in the person *behind* the vision. The same is true for your customers and the people who will eventually join your team. They want to see your vision, but they also need to believe in *you*.

Invite people to imagine a world where you've achieved your vision and talk about why this potential world matters to you. When I share my goals, I paint a vivid picture of that world. I explain what I'm doing to make it a reality, followed by why it matters to me and why I care so deeply about it.

'Imagine' is my favorite word, because it carries incredible power. When you ask someone to imagine and then paint a vivid picture for them, their preconceived ideas momentarily fade away. This creates an opportunity to fill their mind with any vision you want, as long as you can help them truly see it.

To make that vision tangible, you must describe it with vivid detail and rich color. The more realistic the picture, the more it resonates—not just for them, but for you as well. When the mind envisions a future, it begins to believe it's real because we're conditioned to think we only see what already exists. Suddenly, the world you've created for them feels real, and they become inspired to invest in making it happen.

The next powerful tool in this process is invoking: "What if?"

Here's an example from my work at Viome: I start by saying to my audience, "Imagine living in a world where illness is optional." Then I ask, "What if this was possible?" At that point, we show them why it's possible and how we will make it happen. Use the magical little phrase "It turns out that..." to explain a new truth or solution. I explain, "It *is* possible. It turns out that by collecting massive amounts of dynamic data from a large population and leveraging AI, we can uncover the mechanisms behind health changes and pave the way for transformative solutions." Now, they have a complete picture of the vision and the roadmap to get there.

So, if you're painting the picture for your business or any initiative you want people to collaborate with you on, it goes like this:

1. Imagine...

2. What if...

3. It turns out that...

My oldest son Ankur used this formula when he started his company Bilt.

He started with a very simple idea: *Imagine a world where every renter is rewarded for being a renter.*

Then, he would explain: "Today, renters feel stupid for wasting money on rent. They're not getting closer to owning a home or enjoying the benefits of earning points on their credit cards."

Ankur found it exciting that people could earn something back for everyday expenses like dining out or filling up on gas. However, he couldn't understand why paying rent—a major monthly expense—didn't offer the same opportunity. After digging deeper, he discovered the issue: landlords have little incentive to accept credit card payments because they're required to pay a 2.5% to 3% transaction fee to the card companies. As a result, renters are often forced to use the landlord's preferred payment method (check or cash, etc.), limiting their options to earn rewards.

Ankur wondered, *what if credit card companies waived fees for rent payments?* This would enable them to process billions of dollars' worth of payments while still making money on transactions other than rent. It would also allow all renters to earn points by paying rent with a credit card. Landlords could promote a credit card as a default payment method, giving them guaranteed money faster. He wanted to solve this problem for everyone in his generation who can't afford to buy a house.

As you can see, sharing what you're working on doesn't have to be intimidating or overwhelming. If you've done the work to think it through, your confidence will naturally follow. All you need is to share your passion and vision from the heart. When people feel your authenticity, they'll want to join you. You'll attract top experts, investors, and customers alike.

When you embrace this approach, you'll realize that relationships are the key to unlocking abundance in every area of your life. Investing time in meeting great people and collaborating with them isn't just important—it should be a central focus.

Principle 2: Focus on relationships to unlock abundance in all areas

There's an old saying, "If you want to go fast, go alone. But if you want to go far, then go with friends." I couldn't agree more. You can't achieve anything truly significant on your own. Like raising a child, any major undertaking takes a village.

From a business perspective, success is built on people working together. Every business is made up of teams, and at its core, every business is about people. Revenue is generated by offering products or services to others, and connections are the bridge between you (and your team) and your customers. To build those connections effectively, you must first understand people.

But this idea goes beyond business. People are the essence of life itself.

They're why we're here—to connect, support, and help one another grow. A loving, supportive environment gives us the confidence and security we need to take on big challenges and accomplish great things.

In the rush of daily life, it's easy to neglect these connections. You might skip a lunch walk with a colleague, pass on a meeting you deem unimportant, or spend time scrolling through your phone instead of being fully present. Often, the most impactful action—choosing to connect, perhaps even in person rather than virtually—is the one we're least likely to prioritize.

Building and nurturing connections with people of *all kinds* is invaluable. From mentors who can guide you, to junior team members who bring fresh ideas, to customers who have a complaint or a suggestion, every relationship holds potential. When you pause to connect, you unlock the following three benefits:

- Build social capital

- Community provides immunity

- Improved quality of life

Let's delve into each of these points to understand why sometimes choosing an interaction over solitary work is the better path forward.

Build social capital

Social capital, which is the value derived from relationships and networks, can often be transformed into tangible life benefits. A strong network gives you opportunities and access to ideas, partnerships, and new markets.

Trust and good relationships within these networks reduce costs by minimizing the need for excessive oversight, contracts, or insurance, as trustworthy partners are less likely to default or exploit agreements. Additionally, a well-established network enhances reputation and credibility, attracting clients, investors, and collaborators. Referrals and word-of-mouth endorsements, for instance, can directly drive revenue. Social networks also foster the exchange of ideas and knowledge, paving the way for innovation and competitive advantages.

These principles play out in practical scenarios. A small business owner might leverage a loyal network of customers and peers to expand their brand, boosting both sales and profitability. On an individual level, strong social ties can lead to business opportunities, mentorship, or investment advice, enhancing personal wealth and career prospects.

In communities, particularly in underprivileged areas, strong social networks often lead to collective resource pooling, enabling the creation of economic opportunities such as cooperatives or shared ventures. These examples illustrate how social capital directly impacts financial success, highlighting the immense value of investing in relationships and trust. Beyond financial and practical advantages, genuine relationships also offer significant emotional benefits, fostering a sense of belonging, support, and well-being.

Community provides immunity

Community serves as a shield against life's challenges and stresses. When you have people who matter to you—those with whom you feel safe—you gain emotional support, practical resources, and a sense of belonging. A strong social network helps you navigate difficulties with greater resilience.

Being part of a supportive community reduces feelings of isolation. It provides encouragement during tough times, boosting your overall well-being and reinforcing the idea that collective strength can buffer individual struggles. A simple piece of advice from a friend can get you through a difficult moment. Deep relationships are a lifeline, especially when you're pursuing a massive moonshot mission in the world.

Building a small number of deep, meaningful connections is far more valuable than collecting a long list of casual acquaintances. Some people believe that handing out more business cards or shaking more hands at an event leads to better opportunities. I see it differently. If you leave an event with more than a couple of connections, it's likely you didn't build any real relationships.

To nurture relationships that truly propel you toward greatness, abandon the mindset of transactional networking. Instead, focus on having in-depth, authentic conversations with a select few about topics you genuinely care about. Taking off the mask and speaking openly about your life and family can often be more impactful than pitching your business. True connections are built on authenticity, not superficial exchanges.

Improved quality of life

When you have a network of people with whom you feel safe, understood, and connected, your quality of life significantly improves. Relationships add depth and color to our experiences, providing a sense of fulfillment and purpose. In fact, relationships are so essential that numerous studies identify them as a key factor in determining a person's longevity.

Principle 3: Build lasting relationships, not transactions, and know the difference

Whenever I work with people, I avoid treating interactions as mere transactions. Instead, I focus on building relationships and partnerships that last far beyond the lifespan of any single company. Companies may come and go, but true friendships and strong partnerships stand the test of time.

When you're in a position of power, treating others with kindness and fairness creates a foundation of trust and goodwill. One day, those same people may extend a helping hand when you need it most.

When I worked at Microsoft, Windows dominated the global computer market, with over 90% of users on the platform, while Apple's Mac had less than 4% market share. Windows came with Internet Explorer, and every time someone opened it, it defaulted to

MSN.com, which was one of the most visited websites in the world. I was responsible for building partnerships for MSN.com, and because of its massive traffic, I could have charged companies almost anything to feature their services.

At the time, there were only a handful of search engine providers. These companies were eager to grow, and I had the leverage to demand substantial payments. But instead of exploiting that power, I sat down with each company and asked, "How do you plan to monetize this? For every user we send you, how will you generate revenue? Let's figure out a fair deal where you make money, and we also get a portion of that success."

These fair and thoughtful agreements laid the foundation for lasting relationships. About a year later, when I left Microsoft to start my own company, I suddenly needed distribution for my new service and turned to those same companies for help. To my surprise, every single one of them signed a deal with me within the first 30 days. Just as I had with them, they were keen to work out a deal from which we both benefited.

This experience reaffirmed a universal truth: the energy you put into the world comes back to you.

The lesson here is simple: don't focus solely on transactions. Invest in building relationships and friendships that go beyond the immediate business deal. These relationships can create opportunities and goodwill that last a lifetime.

I apply this approach to everything I do—focusing on partnerships, friendships, and relationships rather than pure transactions. Of course, there are people who operate solely on transactions, and that's fine, as long as the boundaries are clear. If it's purely transactional, set the expectation: "This is a transaction. Don't ask me for favors, and I won't ask you for any." That's perfectly acceptable when defined upfront.

Think of it this way: you walk into a store to buy a bottle of water priced at $5. You know it normally costs $2, but you need it, so you pay $5. That's a transaction. But if the store overcharges you unfairly, you're unlikely to return. That's the nature of transactional relationships—once they're over, they're over.

In contrast, partnerships and friendships operate on a completely different level. True partnerships are built on trust, mutual respect, and shared goals, and they endure far beyond any single deal or project. It's essential to surround yourself with people who value meaningful relationships over quick transactions.

The ultimate goal is to cultivate lasting friendships—connections that may start professionally but grow into personal and lifelong bonds. These relationships transcend work and deals, becoming something you can cherish for years to come.

Principle 4: To be unstoppable, fall in love with yourself

The day you fall in love with yourself is the day the world begins to fall in love with you. Self-belief stems from self-love. In the end, all you truly have is yourself, so you might as well choose to embrace and believe in who you are.

If you can't love yourself, how can you expect someone else to love you? Why would anyone else believe in you if you don't believe in yourself? Fulfill yourself first, and you won't need others to fill the gaps. When you do this, you'll attract incredible people and bring more of what you want into your life. While self-love might seem complicated or out of reach, it's actually quite simple.

Loving, trusting, and respecting yourself is about *acceptance*. It's about being real with where you are and who you are in this moment and acting from a place of ownership. Here's a simple exercise you can use anytime to center yourself and act with conviction:

Spend one to three minutes telling yourself your own story. Recount everything that you are grateful for and things that you need to improve to be even better.

For example, here's me:

> I work at Viome. I have an incredible wife, Anu, and three kids. Today, I have a meeting with a potential business partner that I'm both excited and a little nervous about. I come from an immigrant family with very few resources as we were growing up, but God has been really kind to us. I am so proud of the amazing things our kids are doing to solve audacious challenges with their respective ventures.

Be sure to include things you might not feel great about, but state them without moral judgment—just as facts. For example:

> I stepped on the scale this morning, and I am starting to lose some muscle mass. I really need to find time to focus on doing strength training three or four times a week and not just twice a week.

This exercise is about self-ownership. It's about owning both the good and the bad, and you'll find that when you do this, you naturally become matter-of-fact about yourself. That gives you a sense of grounded power.

The more you simply state the facts about who you are—what's working and what's not—without labeling them as good or bad, the more you'll claim ownership of your present self. Done well, this practice gives you immediate power by helping you recognize and fully stand in who you are and who you are not.

Self-belief and self-love are internal processes. When you constantly seek someone else's approval, you hand over control of your happiness to others. Instead, be real about who you are. This honesty allows you to fully own the best parts of yourself and project trustworthiness and respect to the world.

Claim who you are so you can share your unique genius, skills, and gifts with others. If you don't, you'll always look to others for fulfillment and never feel truly relaxed or confident. But if you embrace yourself unapologetically and act from that place, you'll find it far easier to achieve powerful results.

When you are fully you, standing in your truth, the world responds in kind, and achieving your goals becomes a natural extension of who you are.

Ask for what you want

Early in my career, landing a cushy job at Microsoft was neither planned nor predictable. Anu wanted to visit Seattle for a vacation, but I was hesitant about spending too much money. To make the trip more justifiable, I put together a list of companies based in Seattle and, without telling Anu, sent out my resume in the hopes that one of them might invite me for an interview—and cover our travel expenses.

Microsoft was the first to respond. Just a few days after faxing my resume, I received a call from their headquarters and arranged an interview. The following week, Anu and I were on a flight, ready for both a vacation and a potential career-changing opportunity.

At the time, I liked my job and wasn't considering leaving, and I did tell the recruiter at Microsoft about it. I also said that I was curious about the company and thought it wouldn't hurt to get a peek behind the curtain. So, they paid for the trip, and we traveled to Seattle.

Microsoft's interview process at the time involved short sessions with seemingly everyone in the company. It wasn't until the afternoon, however, that you met with anyone with any hiring power. This elaborate vetting process meant that higher-ups never met with anyone unless that person had been thoroughly evaluated and recommended. Executives who did the hiring were fanatical about preserving the culture of the company. So, once you walked into the final interview in the afternoon, the question wasn't whether or not you were going to get an offer, it was how much that offer would be. At the time, this was an extremely rare practice. In most companies you'd sit for one, maybe two interviews and then they'd get back to you days later with an offer.

It's incredibly important, when going through any interview process, negotiation, or partnership, to know the structure of the company you're dealing with. Had I not taken the time to speak with friends of mine who worked or had worked at Microsoft, I would have been on the defensive throughout the series of meetings. Instead, I was in a position of relative strength.

I wasn't particularly invested in whether I got that job or not. Just like with the aptitude test at IIT, I was fully prepared to accept the possibility of failure. Disappointment and unhappiness come from unmet expectations, but since I had none, the Microsoft interview—like the IIT test—felt more like an exercise, even a game.

This mindset left me incredibly relaxed. Without expectations or a fear of failure, I was completely at ease. This gave me an edge: I could confidently make the demands I wanted, knowing I had no problem walking away if they weren't met. Sometimes, approaching a situation as if you have nothing to lose can be the most powerful negotiating tool. Always assert yourself.

In my afternoon meeting, I sat down with a senior executive to discuss a potential role as a program manager. At Microsoft, program managers serve as the bridge between the coders who write software and the executives who make high-level strategic decisions.

The primary responsibility of a program manager is to translate business inputs and needs into clear specifications, oversee the development process, and ensure the final product is delivered on time and according to plan. This role requires a balanced understanding of the coding process to effectively collaborate with developers, as well as a solid grasp of marketing and business demands to align technical efforts with organizational goals.

This role was a perfect fit for me. I had some programming experience from my time at Burroughs, but I was also starting to explore marketing at my current company. This meant I could understand the micro-level concerns of the code warriors at Microsoft while also grasping functionality and marketing on a broader scale.

I'd always been drawn to marketing because it's fundamentally about people. Business—and entrepreneurship especially—is ultimately about understanding people, because success depends on identifying and solving your customers' needs. This job at Microsoft represented my big opportunity to transition from being a technical guy to becoming a businessman.

The interviewer asked me a few questions about my background and about my knowledge of Microsoft's operations. It mostly felt like small talk, until he said, "Naveen, we'd like to give you a job."

"I already have a job," I said.

"So, what would you like us to do?" he asked.

When you're an immigrant and trying to improve your language skills, sometimes you pick up your most colorful phrases from movies. After all, it's the quickest way to learn expressions and idioms that you can be sure someone you are speaking to will understand. So, I said, "Make me an offer I can't refuse." While I didn't deliver my adaptation of Marlon Brando's line with the same swagger that he had in *The Godfather*, I made my point.

The interviewer looked at me and mentioned a salary. It was more than I was earning at my current company, but no one has ever been kicked out of an interview room for negotiating beyond the first offer.

In *The Godfather*, no one would dare present anything but their best offer to Don Corleone, seated behind his mahogany desk, streaks of grey in his hair, dressed in a fine Italian suit, and flanked by imposing, armed bodyguards. But this wasn't *The Godfather*. I wasn't a powerful don—I was just a skinny Indian kid in an off-the-rack, untailored suit. Microsoft's profits would have been perfectly fine without me.

Still, looking him squarely in the eye, I said what Don Corleone's enemies never did: "I absolutely *can* refuse that offer."

We both laughed. I doubt he saw many people on the other end of his desk who were so straightforward and at the same time weren't jumping at the chance to work for Microsoft. He upped his offer by

50% and I accepted it. Anu and I moved up to Seattle before the end of the month.

At that moment, I chose to be unapologetically myself. I wasn't elegant or perfectly polished—I was a clumsy young man simply asking for what I wanted. I shared my truth, letting them know I already had a job, and that honesty made me even more appealing to Microsoft. It was a powerful lesson, one I hope resonates with you: you can simply just be you.

You don't need to pretend or mold yourself into someone else's expectations. Instead, take a moment to reflect on what you truly want and the dreams you hold close. Then, boldly make those desires known. You'll discover that the universe has a way of aligning in your favor. People will show up. They'll feel your authenticity, connect with your vision, and want to help you bring it to life.

There's nothing more powerful than embracing who you are—your strengths and imperfections—and sharing that with the world. When you do, you might just find yourself leading the charge, living out a dream you're creating one step at a time. And when you reach that point, your authenticity will matter more than ever, because the next generation will be looking to you for inspiration on how to live boldly and truthfully—and how to make the world better.

Conventional thought trap

People believe they need to show up perfect and polished so that people will accept them.

Counterintuitive approach

The more you own who you are, accepting your imperfections alongside your positive qualities, the more people will be drawn to you. They will see you as confident, smart, and enjoyable to be around. More opportunities and fulfillment will come to you as a result.

CHAPTER 10

COUNTERINTUITIVE GIVING

"We make a living by what we get. We make a life by what we give."

—Winston Churchill

I WAS IN THE middle of a multi-million-dollar deal when I got a call from an unknown number. I had a gut feeling I should answer it. I did, and it was a call that changed my life.

My partners and I were deep into discussions about taking Intelius—our background check and public records company—public. We had all been through an IPO before, so while the process wasn't new, the intensity was the same as ever. This decision would reshape Intelius, the $100m-revenue company we had built from scratch, and I was buzzing with anticipation. When my phone rang, the woman on the line introduced herself with an air of familiarity, as though we had known each other for years, but I couldn't place her name. She spoke gently but urgently, explaining that her husband had suffered a heart attack and was in the ICU in New Jersey. Despite his situation, he wanted to speak to me. She didn't say why, and I didn't ask.

At first, I hesitated. Was she looking for money? Over the years, I'd received my fair share of calls from people looking for help. She asked if I'd speak to her husband, and I realized this was my last chance to brush her off. My partners were waiting, and something in her tone sounded genuine. I couldn't shake the feeling that I needed to take the call. So, I waited. When he came on, he said, "Naveen, it's Jay."

Hearing his name opened a flood of memories. Jay and I had worked together nearly 30 years ago at Burroughs, one of the pioneers of computing. Jay hadn't been my direct boss, but he had become a mentor, guiding me both professionally and personally as I adjusted to life in a new country.

Listening to him now, as he lay in a hospital bed, I could sense he wasn't calling out of nostalgia. He wasn't seeking sympathy or favors. All he wanted was to check in, see how I was doing, and for me to know how proud he was with all that I had achieved. His sincere joy in my well-being caught me off guard. I felt a pang of shame, realizing I had wondered if he was calling for money. In truth, he was there to remind me of something I had nearly forgotten.

Thirty years earlier, Jay had urged me to stay in the U.S., saying, "Naveen, you're too smart to go back home." It wasn't an insult to India—he simply saw an opportunity for me here. As a young man with a short-term work visa, the idea of building a life in the U.S. seemed like a fantasy. But Jay had opened doors for me, introducing me to contacts in the Bay Area in California who could sponsor my visa and give me a chance. His belief in me had changed my life, setting me on the path that eventually led to my success.

As we talked, he didn't ask about my company or financial achievements. Instead, he asked about my wife, my children, and my family back in India. It was clear that he measured success by a different standard—one rooted in balance, fulfillment, and harmony. To him, success wasn't defined by wealth or power, but by the depth of one's relationships and the values they held dear.

When we hung up, I was left with a profound sense of gratitude. Jay had reached out, from a hospital bed no less, not because he wanted anything, but because he cared. It was a reminder that the most selfless gestures come from those who expect nothing in return. Jay had helped me see potential in myself that I hadn't recognized, and here he was again, helping me reflect on what truly mattered.

Later, as I rejoined my colleagues, the energy in the room shifted for me. Yes, we were in the middle of a massive business deal, but my thoughts were with Jay. Instead of going out to celebrate the prospect of a public offering that night, I went home. I spent the evening with my wife and children, thinking about how I could honor the impact Jay had made in my life.

It soon became clear that the best way to honor Jay was to pay it forward. Jay had given me a gift—the courage to pursue a life I hadn't imagined. Now, I realized, it was my turn to do the same for others.

As we reach the end of this book, I hope the lessons I've shared inspire you to think differently, to see beyond the ordinary, and to pursue the impossible. There is something within each of us—a drive to create, to contribute, to leave something meaningful behind. I urge you to follow that call. Get greedy about it. Indulge in it. And take action to build something the world needs. In doing so, you'll find that life expands in remarkable ways.

But there is one last thing you need to really live your best life: an abundant mindset. The biggest secret to business and life success is that *givers get*. Contribution is everything, so in this final section, I'll share the insights I've gained along the way that seem counterintuitive but will get you to a seven-figure business level and beyond, while living a life of similar magnitude.

Abundance or scarcity mindset? You choose

Everything we think is scarce today is abundant. It is our mindset that makes us believe it is not. People fight over land on Earth, but if you look up, you see that we are a tiny part of our solar system. Our solar system is a tiny part of our galaxy, which is infinitesimally small in the scope of our universe, and our universe may not be much bigger within the scope of the multiverse. Where is the scarcity?

Anytime you feel stuck in life, it is only because you are stuck in a scarcity mindset and need to reflect on the abundant world you are actually living in.

Many people fall into the pit of believing that if someone else has something, it means they cannot have it. This belief is rooted in the assumption that resources are finite, creating a zero-sum, win-lose perspective. However, the truth is that we live in a universe where nothing inherently needs to be scarce. The perception of scarcity is simply a belief system. When you recognize that scarcity is not the truth of reality you can free yourself from that limiting mindset.

Now, if the world is abundant by nature, you might wonder why it is so easy to fall into a scarcity mindset. It is because of our biological hardwiring. Our brains haven't evolved since we were living in the savannas of Africa. Our ancestors faced real scarcity of food, water, and other essentials. Survival depended on recognizing and responding to limited resources. This reality fostered a mindset that prioritized immediate, local survival.

Our brains are wired to focus on negative situations, people, and stimuli in our environment because missing them can lead to potential danger for us. In prehistoric times, failing to notice the rustle of a predator stalking through bushes could result in death. Conversely, missing a positive opportunity rarely had life-threatening consequences. This emphasis on negativity became hardwired into our brains, specifically in the amygdala, which constantly scans for threats. This is why, even today, we are attracted to negative news stories.

Yet, despite these evolutionary roots, we live in the most prosperous era in human history. Even the poorest among us often enjoy better living conditions than the wealthiest individuals did a century ago. Still, the scarcity mindset remains ingrained in our DNA, influencing how we perceive value. For example, we assign monetary value to things we consider scarce, like gold, energy, and real estate. On the other hand, no one pays for air because we perceive it as abundant.

Now imagine a world where everything we value—food, energy, housing—exists in abundance. Would these things still hold the same value? Scarcity drives hoarding and competition. People accumulate resources because they believe scarcity increases value. In contrast, when something is abundant, like air, no one hoards it because there's no fear of running out.

The scarcity mindset also tricks us into believing that things will be more valuable tomorrow than they are today. However, an abundance mindset recognizes that innovation and progress consistently make things cheaper and more accessible over time. Technological advancements, for example, have drastically reduced the cost of energy, communication, and transportation.

Ultimately, it's up to us to recognize when we fall into the trap of scarcity thinking. We must make the conscious effort to remember that we have everything we need and that all the opportunities are ahead of us. This helps us to be open and generous people.

There are five signs you may be operating from a scarcity mindset.

The five signs of scarcity mindset

Here are five signs you may be operating from a scarcity mindset:

1. **Believing your situation is permanent:** If you feel trapped and unable to see a way out, you are likely stuck in a scarcity mindset.

2. **Urgency to acquire:** Thinking, *I need this now before someone else gets it*, reflects scarcity-driven thinking.

3. **Jealousy or envy:** Feeling envious of others' success or possessions signals a belief that their gain is your loss.

4. **Lack of generosity:** If you're not sharing, giving, or helping others, it's a sign you fear running out of resources yourself.

5. **Hoarding behavior:** Stockpiling items out of fear they won't be available later indicates a scarcity mindset.

To adopt an abundance mindset, you have to challenge these beliefs. You have to bring yourself back to the truth that resources aren't finite and instead focus on creating more of what you need. You have to remind yourself that the universe is not inherently lacking in resources. Scarcity exists only because of our limited belief systems.

For example, we think land is scarce because Earth is finite, but what if we could live on the Moon, Mars, or beyond? What if the resources we need could be accessed in entirely new ways? This 'what if' thinking fuels creativity and innovation.

No matter what you do and how big you think, there will be times you need to bring yourself out of scarcity and back into abundance. Here are the five practices I encourage you to use when you fall into a scarcity mindset:

1. **Visualize your desired world:** Start by imagining a world of abundance. What would it look like if the things you perceive as scarce were plentiful? Close your eyes and vividly picture the details of this world. The clearer your vision, the easier it becomes to work toward it.

2. **Reframe your current reality:** Analyze your thought process. Are you accepting the world as it is, or envisioning the world as it could be? Recognize that many of the limitations we perceive are self-imposed. By believing in possibilities, you can create solutions that others dismiss as impossible.

3. **Practice gratitude:** Gratitude is a cornerstone of the abundance mindset. Each morning, reflect on what you're thankful for. Celebrate even the smallest blessings, like good health or the presence of loved ones. When you focus on gratitude, you shift your attention from what's lacking to what's already abundant.

4. **Surround yourself with possibilities:** Spend time with people who inspire and challenge you to think bigger. Collaborate with those who share your vision of creating a better world. Smart, driven individuals are drawn to bold ideas, and together, you can achieve the extraordinary.

5. **Meditate and focus:** Daily distractions can cloud your vision and drain your energy. Take two to five minutes each morning and evening to meditate. Focus on your breathing and tune out the noise around you. This practice clarifies your thoughts and channels your energy toward meaningful goals.

Living from abundance is how you live the final principle that 'givers get.' It is the difference between choosing to compete with a person in your industry or taking the perspective that there are enough customers to go around. When choosing the path of abundance, you might even team up and build something better together.

You will find when you live in this way, with the understanding the world is an abundant place, an abundant life is what you get back. When you give without expecting a return you will see that your life opens up and you will feel deep fulfillment.

Give your best stuff away

This might sound counterproductive, but sharing your expertise freely enhances your reputation and attracts clients. Offering value upfront establishes you as a trusted resource in your field. Always share what you know and don't hold back because you are scared someone will steal your intellectual property. If you come from this place you will continue to learn and grow, and everyone can have what they want.

The same is true of people. When you start a company, all you have is an idea and a vision. At that stage, you're not much different from a cult leader. People join you because they believe in you and your vision, much like followers of a cult. However, there's a critical difference between a cult leader and an entrepreneur: cult leaders keep their followers' loyalty focused on themselves. In contrast, as an entrepreneur, your role is to shift the loyalty of your team from yourself to the company and its mission.

Over time, you should become less important as an individual. Let the cause and the organization take center stage. You become just one part of the larger puzzle—a piece of the organism working collectively toward a shared goal. In a great company, the mission and the company itself become the driving force. That's the key difference between a cult and a successful entrepreneur.

In the early days of a company, when it is young, it is like a baby. You have to spend a lot of your energy to nurture it and to help it grow. But as it grows, and money flows in from sales and key employees are hired to tend it, a company starts to become more stable and less fragile. As a baby grows into a child, then a teen, and eventually into young adulthood, it becomes more self-sufficient. It has different needs at each stage of development, but as you provide what it needs it starts to thrive.

Allow your people to grow through your organization, and if the time comes that they want to go off, even if they are tough to replace, let them. Be there to support them as they grow. They might become partners later on.

We are hardwired to protect our self-interests. From a young age, we're taught to compete—to be the best athlete, the top scholar, or the most successful professional. However, we're rarely encouraged to prioritize the interests of others over our own. The idea of sacrificing our desires, fame, or fortune so that someone else can excel is often foreign to us. Yet, if that 'someone else' is our child, we don't think twice about making that sacrifice.

A giver celebrates the success of those around them, encouraging them and genuinely cheering for their achievements. A kind word can make a significant difference in someone's life. Even when you feel like you have nothing to offer, you can always provide support and encouragement. Your words might be the spark that inspires someone to take the next step in their journey toward success.

Also, learn to share your victories. When you achieve something, take time to acknowledge the people who helped you get there. Whether they played a major role or simply supported you from the sidelines, recognize their contribution. This shows that you value them, care about them, and are willing to share the fruits of your success. Building this kind of mutual respect fosters a strong network of people who are committed to both your success and their own.

As you rise to the top, don't lose sight of the challenges faced by those at different levels of the economic ladder. Take a moment to ask yourself: *What can I do to improve their situation?* By cultivating this abundant and giving mindset—one of sharing, encouraging, and lifting others—you'll create a ripple effect of positivity that extends far beyond your immediate circle.

Humility is the true measure of success

We all work hard to achieve progress, but how do you know when you've truly reached success? Financial milestones, like earning a billion dollars, can signal achievement, but the clearest sign is humility. Real success comes the day you no longer feel the need to prove your worth—to the world or to yourself. If even a trace of arrogance remains, there's still room to grow. A life of significance extends beyond financial success.

The day you become humble is the day you become successful. Success shouldn't be defined by money in the bank; it's about how many lives you can positively impact. That's why I say, "The day you become humble is the day you become successful." If any part of you still needs to prove something to yourself or others, the journey isn't complete.

If you find yourself viewing anyone or anything as 'beneath' you, check yourself. There is much to learn from every activity and person. And you will find the learning you need in places you may not expect. This is why whenever I finish speaking at a conference, my next stop is speaking to individual people at the company's booth. There is nothing more important than getting out and talking to customers. This is how you understand what they're dealing with.

To turn a crazy idea into a business that is focused on helping a billion people, you need not only an obsession but also a belief that no detail is too small to deserve your attention. More often than not, especially in the early stages of building a business, companies fail due to overlooking details—not the big picture.

Humility means not needing to tell anyone you're the smartest or the richest. You don't have to prove anything about who you are. That's real success—reaching a place where you do things not to impress but to create real value.

You will see that when you give to the world, it gives back to you. The universe will bring you people and opportunities you could never fathom, and a life more fulfilling than you ever imagined.

Conventional thought trap

It is easy to believe the resources are finite, ideas are scarce, and that you need to look out for yourself by keeping your ideas and gifts quiet.

Counterintuitive approach

The world is an abundant place. Come from that perspective and be someone who gives and contributes. When you live with that mindset, opportunities, financial abundance, and the people you need will flow to you.

CONCLUSION

OVER THE YEARS, I've launched seven companies that have grown to have large enough market capitalizations that I've taken them public. I've ridden the roller coaster of the dot-com boom and bust, experienced the highs and lows of striking out on my own, and along the way, I've learned that success is about far more than the ups and downs of a company's financial performance.

For me, life is about something larger—following an undeniable calling that enables the creation of a meaningful life. And there's a good chance that may be your path as well.

If there is one thing I must do as we reach the end of this book, it is to encourage you to take the entrepreneurial leap. This can look like stepping out on your own and starting a business. It might look like an initiative within a company or a collaboration inside of a community. If you have a dream, take action, become a doer, and live a tremendously fulfilling life. To encourage you, let me reinforce what this journey entails.

Many people have an oversimplified view of entrepreneurship. They see it as a bold journey of self-reliance, leaving behind the security of corporate life to pursue a brilliant idea. In this flat narrative, success is inevitable if you have a great idea and a bit of startup capital. But this couldn't be further from the truth. If you cling too closely to conventional wisdom about entrepreneurship, you'll likely fail. Sure, you'll gain lessons for your next venture, but the odds of success diminish significantly if you buy into this simplified view.

The traditional path emphasizes innovation, a polished business plan, and securing investors. It also suggests that generating buzz matters more than achieving profitability, or even revenue. And even more misleadingly, it treats entrepreneurship solely as a business endeavor, not a life-encompassing journey with profound spiritual and emotional elements. But the reality is that you can't separate your business life from your personal life because, ultimately, you only have one life. The mental challenges, emotional trials, and tedious tasks of running a business inevitably spill into your time. Being an entrepreneur requires a higher level of responsibility.

As an entrepreneur, you're not only responsible for your business and personal life but also the professional and financial growth—and often the personal well-being—of your employees, who may be close friends or even family. It's a responsibility that's always present, so heavy and essential that you can't set it down for a moment without the risk of being unable to pick it up again. For those seeking a clean break from work at 5 pm, this might seem like a burden. But living this way is an absolute blessing.

Entrepreneurship sharpens your mind. You become quicker, more agile, and more insightful simply because you must be. Too many decisions depend on you, and people rely on you.

An entrepreneur is never truly off duty. Even on vacation, if a critical decision arises, it's up to you to make the call that could shape your company's direction and fate. Like a surgeon on call, your mind has to be ready at a moment's notice. And although entrepreneurship is indeed an extreme sport, it teaches you the value of balance and perspective. If you're anxious, overwhelmed, or stressed in your personal life, it affects your company's performance.

Conversely, if you can maintain calm and peace in your personal and spiritual life, it will enable you to lead your company with clarity. The reverse is also true: if your work life is constantly fraught with tension, it seeps into your personal life, and both will suffer.

Finding a balance between personal life and business is unattainable. First of all, the very idea of *balancing* implies that you've already concluded the two can't coexist in harmony. But life and business aren't opposing forces. They're in a relationship. Some days, one will demand more of your time; other days, the other will. Anyone who claims they've found the perfect balance is likely failing at both. Their spouse probably feels they aren't spending enough time at home, while their business suffers from a lack of dedication. It's important to understand that life and business ebb and flow and to navigate that dynamic with intention.

Entrepreneurship has made me a better person and given me a better life. I have learned that when you create incredible things and move ideas forward, not only do you live out your dreams but you leave legacy behind.

The bottom line

In the end, no matter what else you do, be someone who *creates* and *takes action*. Solve big problems that impact large groups of people. This is what it means to truly live. To follow your dreams and create new incredible things in this world is challenging, but it is deeply worth it. You will feel a fulfillment you have never felt before.

Now you have a roadmap. And you know what you need to do next:

Take action.

ACKNOWLEDGMENTS

MEANINGFUL PROGRESS doesn't happen in isolation, and transformative ideas only come to life through people willing to question the status quo and think differently *together*. Counterintuitive ideas often begin as fragile sparks, but it takes belief, collaboration, and shared courage to help them survive and grow into something real. This book is the result of many such minds, conversations, challenges, and acts of support. I am deeply grateful to those who have walked this journey with me, and what follows is a small expression of thanks to the people who made it possible.

First and foremost, to my wife and partner, Anu: it is a privilege to build, dream, and explore this journey with you by my side. Thank you for your patience, wisdom, grounding presence, and for believing in me and my ideas.

To my children, Ankur, Priyanka, and Neil: watching you grow into thoughtful leaders, entrepreneurs, and changemakers has been one of my greatest joys. I look forward to continuing to learn from one another as we mentor, challenge, and support each other through our respective ventures.

To my colleagues, collaborators, and industry peers—from my early days at Microsoft and InfoSpace, through Moon Express, and to my work at Viome today—thank you. Your insights, dedication, and willingness to push boundaries have shaped both my thinking and my outcomes. I have learned from more people than I can name, and this life would not have been possible without you.

To my writing partner and collaborators who helped bring this book into existence: I am grateful to Kay Walker, my book collaborator, and Andy Walker, development editor, from the Cyberwalker Media team. Your ability to help me shape my ideas and share them with the world has been invaluable.

To the publishing team at Harriman House of Macmillan Publishing: To my editor, Nick Fletcher, thank you for your editorial insight and guidance. You knew what this book needed to reach its full potential.

And finally, to you, the reader: thank you for your curiosity and your willingness to question what you've been taught. By opening this book, you've already taken the first step toward thinking differently. I hope these pages encourage you to trust your ideas, act on them, and give them the chance to survive.

If you apply what you learn here, I know you'll discover what I have: the extraordinary is far more accessible than you were ever led to believe.

ABOUT THE AUTHOR

NAVEEN JAIN is an innovative entrepreneur dedicated to tackling global challenges. He founded several successful companies, including Moon Express, which aims to harvest lunar resources and enable multi-planetary living, and Viome, which seeks to make illness elective through personalized nutrition based on microbial insights.

Naveen also serves on the board of the X PRIZE Foundation, where he champions incentive prizes—like the Women Safety XPRIZE— to solve societal issues. He is also a board member at Singularity University, focused on empowering leaders to address humanity's grand challenges with technology.

He has received numerous accolades for his work, including Ernst & Young Entrepreneur of the Year, the Albert Einstein Technology Medal, and the Ellis Island Medal of Honor.